TO: Ror...

CW00762264

ULSTER

Slemish
(site of Patrick's Captivity)

Antrim

Armagh

Saul
(Downpatrick)

Croagh
Patrick

CONNAUGHT

Oran
(Uaran Gar)

Telltown

Trim

Tara

Clonmacnoise

MEATH

Lough
Derg

Wicklow
(Inver Dea)
Patrick's first
landing

LEINSTER

Crosspatrick

Cashel

MUNSTER

_ Words I don't understand

ST. PATRICK APOSTLE OF IRELAND

S·PATRICIVS S·MARTINVS

S: PATRICK AND S: MARTIN OF TOURS
(FLANDRIN.)

St. Patrick
Apostle of Ireland

The Notre Dame Series of Lives of the Saints

PUBLISHED BY SANDS & COMPANY 1911

2011
St. Augustine Academy Press
Lisle, Illinois

This book is newly typeset based on the 1911 edition published by Sands & Company. All editing strictly limited to correcting errors in the original text and the addition of appendix material.

Nihil Obstat
GEORGIUS H. BENNETT, S.T.D.
Censor Deputatus.

Imprimatur
+JACOBUS AUGUSTINUS,
Archiep. S. And-et Edimburgen.

EDIMBURGI, *die 16 Maii 1911.*

This book was originally published in 1911 by Sands & Company.
This edition ©2011 by St. Augustine Academy Press.
All editing by Lisa Bergman.

ISBN: 978-1-936639-10-6
Library of Congress Control Number: 2012935586

Unless otherwise noted, all illustrations in this book, including the cover,
are either the original illustrations as found in the book,
or are public domain images.
Map of Ireland on inside cover by Lisa Bergman.

Contents

Editor's Note

HE present volume was first published in 1911 by Sands & Company as part of the "Notre Dame Series of Lives of the Saints." However, the fact that its title is far from unique, and that no Author's name is associated with it, makes it difficult to set it apart from the many other works written about this popular saint.

We have chosen to reprint this particular title because, of those we have seen, it presents the story of St Patrick in the best possible way: that is, it relies as much as possible on primary sources such as Patrick's own *Confession* and *St. Fiacc's Hymn*, and makes use of those parts of the *Tripartite Life* that are most aligned with these, while omitting those parts which smack of hyperbole or outright fable. Nor does it treat these latter with condescension, but as the author states in the preface, "its principal object is to introduce the inexperienced reader to the study of St Patrick's life and times in such a manner that, should he be tempted to pursue that study further, he may at least find nothing of importance to unlearn." The result is a very straightforward, readable narrative that is neither overly scholarly nor overly fanciful.

In addition, those who would like to be able to consult Patrick's original *Confession* will find that the three documents which we can reliably attribute to St Patrick have been added as an Appendix. Here, in addition to the *Confession*, can be found

"*St Patrick's Breastplate*"—the hymn he is said to have sung at Tara—and Patrick's *Epistle to Coroticus.*

But one of the more valuable parts of this book for the Catholic family are the illustrations. In this day and age, where all of our St Patrick's Day decorations consist of Leprechauns and four-leafed clovers, it is often hard to come by any images of this most famous saint. Those that can be found invariably show him in the full—GREEN—regalia of a bishop, pointing threateningly at a few snakes. And while the illustrations within may not be any more accurate representations of the real St Patrick, they at least present a more realistic vision of one of the greatest misssionary saints the world has known.

Lisa Bergman
St. Augustine Academy Press
March 2011

PREFACE

T HE following pages are based on the documents edited by Dr Whitley Stokes for the Rolls Series under the title of "The Tripartite Life of Patrick and other Documents relating to that Saint." The quaint phraseology of the original narrative is frequently retained even without indication by inverted commas; while all cases of direct speech are taken literally from the text.

The "Legends of St Patrick," by Aubrey de Vere, have been freely used without other reference to their author than this general acknowledgment.

Those who are acquainted with the sources can realise how much this little book owes to the guidance of Archbishop Healy. His "Life and Writings of St Patrick," with its invaluable topographical information, its scholarly interpretation of theological and liturgical difficulties, and its large grasp of the ecclesiastical history of the period, has been closely followed.

The present volume, while not ignoring criticism, does not claim to be critical. It consists merely of the old stories retold, as far as may be in the light of modern research; and its principal object is to introduce the inexperienced reader to the study of St Patrick's life and times in such a manner that, should he be tempted to pursue that study further, he may at least find nothing of importance to unlearn.

The Baptism of St. Patrick.

Chapter I

St Patrick's Childhood

St Patrick was born of noble and Christian parents towards the close of the fourth century. His father, Calpurnius, though of British race, was by birth a Roman citizen, and held the rank of decurion or member of the corporation of his native town. The father and grandfather of Calpurnius, Potitus and Odissus, had both been Christians, so that the family had kept the faith for at least several generations.

Tradition tells us that Conchessa, Patrick's mother, was a near relative of the great St Martin of Tours. She was a wise and holy woman, and, in union with her husband, sought to bring up their children in the fear and love of God. Their two sons, Patrick and Sannan, and their five daughters, walked in the footsteps of their parents, and all became great servants of God and His Church. But Patrick so far eclipsed his brethren that he deserved to be spoken of by an old chronicler in the following beautiful words:—

"There lay great darkness and gloom over the hearts of the

heathen until the Sun of Justice, Jesus Christ, scattered His radiance over the quarters of the globe, to enlighten it through His apostles, and through His saints and just men, and also through their holy successors.

One, then, of the rays and of the flames which the Sun of Justice, Jesus Christ, sent into the world—the ray and the flame, and the precious stone, and the brilliant lamp, which lighted the west of the world—is holy Patrick, high bishop of the west, and father of the baptism and belief of the men of Ireland."

Calpurnius dwelt at Bannavem Taberniae, the exact situation of which has been the subject of much discussion. But whether it was near the rock of Dumbarton, or in Wales, or on the lower Severn, or at Boulogne, we must leave scholars to determine. It was certainly in some part of Roman Britain or Brittany, on the shore of the "Western Sea," and near a river mouth. Many places have been pointed out, but none has yet proved its claim to be that of Patrick's birth. That he was chosen by God, and endowed with all the natural and supernatural gifts essential to his mission, is all that concerns us here.

This was the view taken by the ancient Irish teachers, who did not hesitate to surround the actions and character of their great Apostle with a tissue of legends in which it is impossible at the present day to distinguish reality from imagination. The only reliable historical document we possess is the "Confession" of St Patrick, written by himself towards the close of his life. Ancient biographies of him there are in plenty, but none composed until three or four centuries after his death. Of these the most important and interesting is the "Tripartite Life," so called because it consists of three parts. It is in Irish, interspersed with passages in Latin, and many of the quaint expressions in the following pages are due to close translation of the original manuscripts, which were written before the Anglo-Norman invasion of Ireland.

Grave historians of modern times have been sadly perplexed by the strange and often incredible stories in which the Tripartite abounds, in common with the other ancient lives of St Patrick. And we ourselves may be puzzled to reconcile our ideas of the Christian meekness and gentleness of the true apostle with some features of our Saint's character as he is represented in his missionary journeys, working miracles to terrify and subdue the enemies of the faith. St Patrick's right hand was often raised to bless, but, according to the chroniclers, his terrible left hand was just as often lifted to bring down a curse upon the wicked.

It is clear that in these stories there is some misrepresentation or distortion of the truth. The blame of this may be laid at the door of the poets and bards who lived and sang during the Saint's life and immediately after his death. He had converted them to Christianity, it is true, but they had not forgotten the pagan traditions of their art. They, therefore, represented their hero as a man of might, opposing the magic practices of druids and sorcerers by prompt and destructive miracles.

Patrick was to them a worker of wonders, endowed from his very cradle with supernatural powers. Bard vied with bard in investing even his earliest years with a halo of sanctity of their own invention, such as Patrick himself lays no claim to in his writings; a sanctity, which, in fact, he strongly denies.

But these poetic extravagances took firm root among the people, and came to be believed even by the learned, who had no other information at hand. Hence we find serious biographers of St Patrick, such as the authors of the Tripartite Life, setting down fables and legends as facts. Hence, also, the impossibility of distinguishing between allegory and sober history, so that we now find ourselves under the necessity of simply reproducing our materials in the form in which they have been handed down to us.

That St Patrick worked great and wonderful miracles is beyond question. That they were such miracles as to have their share in winning for him the enthusiastic admiration and the enduring love of his people is equally certain. Still, for the miracles of his childhood, for example, we have slight authority. God could have bestowed the powers ascribed to him, and may have done so in view of his future sanctity. Our Lady appeared to the little girl, Bernadette, and the miracles of Lourdes are with us to-day. The child, Gerard Majella, was favoured with gifts not surpassed by his miracles as a canonised saint.

So, whether historical or not, these stories of St Patrick, coming down to us as they do from remote antiquity, claim our respectful attention. Their origin is lost in the mists of that far-off time when Ireland's soil had been but lately trodden by the blessed feet of him who preached the gospel of peace to a grateful people; and when the shamrock, fresh from his holy hands, spoke in never-to-be-forgotten language of the truths of faith. Just as the shamrock symbolises the Three Persons in One God, so do these legends of St Patrick symbolise his gracious personality and his noble work.

We gather these anecdotes together, therefore, in order that, catching from them some of the narrator's strong faith in the character of his hero, we may reverently gaze upon what they reflect of the saintly Apostle, who, like his Divine Master, went about doing good and teaching souls the way to heaven. We may thus form for ourselves a picture such as de Vere suggests:—

> "Beholding not alone his wondrous works,
> But, wondrous more, the sweetness of his strength
> And how he neither shrank from flood nor fire,
> And how he couched him on the wintry rocks,
> And how he sang great hymns to One who heard,
> And how he cared for poor men and the sick,
> And for the souls invisible of men."

The virtues thus described by the poet underlie all the ancient traditions, however much they may seem to be concerned with severe denunciations of wickedness and the execution of terrible threats of punishment for sin.

Miracles presided even over the birth of the Saint. As no priest was to be found, the infant was taken to be baptized by the blind hermit, Gornias, who dwelt in the neighbourhood. A difficulty arose from the want of water with which to perform the ceremony. Gornias, however, inwardly enlightened, took the tiny hand of the babe and with it traced the sign of the cross upon the earth, with the result that a spring of water gushed forth. Bathing his own eyes first, the hermit forthwith saw, and was able to read the baptismal rite, although before this he had been unacquainted with letters. In after years a church, in the form of a cross, was erected on the site of the triple miracle, and all could see the well which stood close by the altar as a memorial of the wonderful event.

In Nemthur, as we learn from "Fiacc's Hymn," under the care of a foster-mother, the boy was brought up. He grew in age, in grace, in good works and in the miracles which God wrought by him.

"For from his childhood he had been endued with God's grace, even before he knew how to discern between good and evil, or was able to trace out the path of truth. As he himself declares in the Book of Epistles, saying, 'And He had pity on my youth and ignorance, and He took care of me before I knew Him, and before I could distinguish between good and evil. And He strengthened me and comforted me as a father does his son.' "

Although of noble birth, the child was not brought up in luxury. His foster-parents are represented as careful, thrifty people, perhaps living on the farm which belonged to Calpurnius, and attending to his flocks and herds. We are first introduced to the good foster-mother in circumstances which would have tried the patience of a saint. The river had overflowed its banks, and the flood poured into the house, lifting on its surface all the lighter articles, so that the vessels and furniture were afloat, and the fire on the hearth was quenched.

In the midst of the confusion the baby Patrick cried for food. But the woman cared little at that moment if the child was hungry.

"We have something else to do," she said, "rather than make food for thee, when not even the fire is alive."

The little boy at once understood the situation. Without a word, he ran to a part of the house which was still dry, and dipping his hand into the water, he held it so that five drops from his fingers fell upon the floor. Straightway the drops became five sparks; the fire blazed up and burnt so fiercely that the water was soon gone. Thus did the child console his foster-mother, and she magnified the name of God for giving him the power to work that miracle.

Again, it was the frosty winter-time, and Patrick was playing with the other children in the snow. Seeing some large icicles he gathered them into the fold of his little tunic, and ran with them to his foster-mother, thinking to give her pleasure. His reception was not such as he had anticipated, and like any other child he must have felt rather crestfallen when he was sharply rebuked for his pains.

"To bring a faggot of firewood that we might warm ourselves thereat were better for us than what thou hast brought."

But he answered sweetly:—

"Believe that it is in the power of God that the icicles should flame like firewood,"—and quicker than speech, when the icicles were set on the fire, and when he had breathed upon them, they flamed forthwith like firewood. God's name and Patrick's were magnified by that miracle.

Once when Patrick was minding sheep with his sister, Lupita, the little girl tripped and fell, striking her head violently against a stone. Her brother was some distance away, but when he returned and found her lying there, as it were dead, he grieved exceedingly. Trusting in God, however, he raised her up, and made the sign of the cross upon the wound. It instantly healed, and the girl came to herself, feeling quite well, but the scar remained visible, as a proof of the miracle. The children returned home together as if nothing had happened.

At another time while Patrick was with the sheep, a wolf came and carried one away. He was severely blamed for his supposed carelessness, but, instead of excusing himself, he prayed earnestly that the loss might be made good. The next day, the wolf brought back the sheep whole and sound, a most unusual proceeding on the part of such an animal, as the chronicler quaintly remarks.

One day Patrick wanted a drink of milk, so his foster-mother went to milk the cow, and the child followed her. But the cow was mad, a demon having entered into it, and it killed five other cows that were with it in the byre. His foster-mother was greatly distressed, but she had by this time learnt to trust in God and Patrick. She told the boy, therefore, to bring the kine back to life. He obeyed, and the mad cow was also cured. In this way God's name and Patrick's were once more magnified.

And thus, from day to day Patrick continued to endear himself to those with whom he dwelt. His foster-mother became so attached to the boy that she could not bear to let him go out of her sight. Hence, on one occasion when the Britons had a great meeting, his foster-parents took him with them. While they were there his foster-father died suddenly. At first, a great hush fell upon the assembly; then the man's kinsfolk began to weep, and his wife wailed aloud, and turning to Patrick, she said:—

St. Patrick Taming the Mad Ox.

"My boy, why hast thou allowed to die the man who was so kind to thee?"

Patrick had been playing with the other children, and had not noticed the distress of the people. Now, however, seeing what had happened, he ran to his foster-father, and putting his arm round the dead man's neck, he said affectionately:—

"Arise, and let us go home."

The man arose at once at Patrick's word, and, full of life and vigour, he returned with his wife and the boy to their own house.

It was the custom of the children of the place in which Patrick was brought up, to seek for honey in the woods, and to bring it to their mothers. His foster-mother said to Patrick:— "Though every child brings honey to his foster-mother, you bring none to me."

Mindful of this reproach, Patrick took a vessel to the well and filled it. On reaching home, he blessed the water, which was turned into miraculous honey having the power to heal every ailment.

The foregoing anecdotes are of no value except in as far as they give some idea of child-life in those early ages and of the view taken by the Irish chroniclers of Patrick's boyhood. According to some critics they should be passed over in silence in any serious biography of the Saint, and we have, in fact, reproduced only a few instances from the Tripartite Life, that our readers may see and judge for themselves.

Fosterage was a custom peculiar to the tribal system of ancient Ireland, and was regulated in all its details by the Brehon laws, which ordained that the sons of nobles should be educated in the homes of the tribesmen until they reached the age of seventeen—the daughters until their fourteenth year. We are, therefore, justified in rejecting these statements as purely legendary, since fosterage could not have affected the family of a Roman citizen. We can only suppose that the bards grafted their own ideas upon whatever scanty traditions they may have been able to glean. The task of disengaging these traditions from the tangled skein of legend has now become impossible.

The general conclusion to be drawn from the stories is, that the Saint was brought up strictly, taught to labour with his hands, and trained to endure privations and hardships with courage. The activity of his temperament, his natural cheerfulness, generosity and kindness of heart, had full scope in the healthy outdoor life he led, while the tender affection of his guardians shielded him from all harm. His mind was already drawn to God by faith and confidence, his conversation was with the angels, and no shadow of evil had yet crossed his path.

As the son of a British noble and a Roman citizen, the boy was bound to receive some literary education. The names bestowed upon him by his parents show that they expected great things of him, and that in the natural course of events, he would one day take up the office of his father, and succeed to his property. According to the custom of British citizens of the Roman Empire, he had three names, rendered in Latin as Patricius, Magonus, Sucatus. The first, Patrick, means noble; the second is of doubtful meaning; while the third, Sucat, is a Celtic name meaning valiant in war.

Although well acquainted with the British tongue, he studied Latin carefully, and probably used it in ordinary conversation, for the Britons of the towns were completely Romanized. Nevertheless, owing to the abrupt cessation of his studies, he never became a Latin scholar, a fact which is well attested by his writings. He most humbly protests in his "Confession" that he is the most uncultured and the least of all the faithful and contemptible in the eyes of many. We know, however, that he was well grounded in the knowledge of Holy Scripture, and though he says that at the age of sixteen he was ignorant of the true God, he can only mean a comparative ignorance due to the thoughtlessness of youth.

He tells us, too, that the people among whom he grew up were disobedient to the dictates of our holy religion, and that, in consequence, they were severely chastised by God. They had strayed away from the right path, refusing to keep the commandments, and resisting their priests, who sought to lead them in the way of salvation. With all the self-abasement of a saint, he confounds himself with his neighbours, taking upon himself the responsibility of their offences against God. And yet he has but one definite fault of his own to reproach himself with, a fault committed before his sixteenth year and bitterly repented of during his whole life. This very fact is a strong testimony to the innocent and holy life he must have led from his earliest years.

The Picts and Scots, of whose invasions we read in history, were the instruments made use of by God to chastise St Patrick's countrymen for their sins. The whole Roman Empire was falling into decay, and barbarians were pressing upon it from every side. Tribes of Germans were pouring into the provinces north of the Danube; Huns and Goths were advancing westward; while every sea-coast was harassed by the light ships of marauders seeking for spoil.

Then it was that from the safe harbours of Ireland her warlike chieftains swooped down upon the unprotected shores of Gaul and Britain. In these hostile raids they generally succeeded in seizing a vast amount of plunder, and many captives whom they sold on their return, in the slave markets of their country.

One of the most powerful and victorious of these sea-kings was Niall, surnamed of the Nine Hostages, because, says the chronicler, he "took hostages from the five provinces of

Ireland, and also French, Saxon, British and Alban hostages."
By some, Niall is thought to have been the means of bringing
the blessed Patrick to the land which he had been destined by
God to evangelize. That land was to be to Patrick as a heritage
for eternity; its people were to be his people, and to him was
to be granted the supreme privilege of joining the ranks of the
Apostles, and of judging the men of Ireland on the great day of
doom.

Chapter II

In Exile and Slavery

HE first sixteen years of Patrick's life went by peacefully in the shelter of his home. But the civilised world was oppressed with a feeling of insecurity. No coast was safe from the depredations of sea-rovers coming from countries beyond the Roman pale. When the catastrophe occurred which was to determine our Saint's destiny, he happened to be at his father's country house, in the company of some of the younger children, and, perhaps, superintending the men and maid-servants who did the farm work.

A sudden alarm was given: strange ships were gliding towards the shore, their crews consisting of armed warriors, whose fierce aspect filled the beholders with terror. Too well did the unfortunate inhabitants realise the meaning of the spectacle. Panic-stricken, they ran hither and thither, but there was little hope of defence or escape. Patrick, like the captain of a sinking ship, remained at his post, directing and commanding as best he could.

With hideous shouts and cries the pirates beached their ships and landed. Some rushed towards the homestead, seeking for objects of value; others laid hands upon the terrified servants and children, and carried them off. An unarmed youth, though ever so brave, would have found himself powerless in the grasp of one of these stalwart barbarians.

In the twinkling of an eye the whole desperate struggle was over. The house was set on fire; the plunder and the captives were hastily thrown into the ships; and Patrick, with his companions, set sail for the land of exile. In vain they strained their eyes to catch a last glimpse of home and fatherland, with, perchance, some lingering hope of rescue. But nothing met their gaze save black smoke rising from devastated buildings; ruin and desolation reigned where an hour ago were peace and plenty.

"They went round Ireland northwards and they landed in the north and sold Patrick to Milcho." This is all we are told, but we can easily picture the horrors of such a voyage: the light boats tossed upon the waves of the mighty Atlantic; the rude, rough men with fierce gestures, shouting their orders in an unknown tongue; the physical torture of bonds and blows, combined with the feeling of blank despair at their hearts, which must have made them long for death.

The ships soon parted company and each sought the port nearest home or where they were most likely to find purchasers of their booty. Patrick disembarked somewhere on the coast of Antrim, and must have been grievously disappointed to find himself separated from his sister Lupita and perhaps from another of his sisters, said to have been carried off at the same time, though in different boats. But there was not much time for reflection. The captives were dragged at once to the slave market where, they were drawn up in line to be examined by intending purchasers.

Patrick's external good qualities soon caught the eye of a petty king of Dalaradia, Milcho by name, who had come to buy slaves and who, after some bargaining, paid the price required. The youth was then led away to his master's fort or dun, in the neighbourhood of the mountain now called Slemish. There he was placed in charge of a herd of swine which fed on the acorns in the adjoining woods. In this occupation his knowledge of outdoor work came to his aid; but the change from his former life was a bitter one and the hardships he endured were extreme. This was, however, the means by which Divine Providence intended him to be prepared for his destined task, and the Saint corresponded faithfully with all the graces he received.

As he performed his menial office he had time for deep thought and earnest prayer, together with the cultivation of profound humility and self-accusation. It was in punishment for his sins, he reflected, and those of his people, that he had been thus cast out among strangers to the "uttermost parts of the earth." To the Roman mind Ireland was literally the most remote portion of the known world, and Patrick does not exaggerate the impression produced upon him by his exile.

But there, he tells us in his "Confession," the Lord opened the understanding of his unbelief, so that at length he might recall to mind his sins and be converted to God. Before he was humbled he was as a stone which is "sunk in the deep mire," but He that is mighty came and lifted him up and placed him "on the top of the wall." "Wherefore," he says, "I cannot conceal, nor indeed, is it fitting that I should conceal the great favours and the great grace which the Lord vouchsafed to bestow upon me in the land of my captivity; for this is the return we make that after our chastening, or after our recognition of God, we should exalt and proclaim His wondrous ways before every nation which is under heaven."

His soul rose to the heights of heavenly contemplation as, from the hilltop of Slemish, his eyes wandered over the lovely landscape or beheld the glories of the rising or setting sun.

Then the words of Holy Scripture which he had learnt all too carelessly in his happy childhood returned to his memory with redoubled force, and in them he found courage and consolation. Often he must have thought over the stories of the ancient patriarchs and prophets, praying to them, as later on, when threatened with danger, he called upon Elias.

But his life was not wholly solitary. In the service of his master he found companions with whom to associate and from them he learnt the Irish language and became intimately acquainted with the manners and customs of the people. Gradually and naturally, yet with a strong supernatural stimulus, he began to yearn for the opportunity of leading the people of this beautiful pagan island to the knowledge of the true God,

His prayers were not only contemplative but also very definite and, probably, vocal. As many as a hundred times during the day, he tells us, he placed himself in the presence of God and addressed petitions to Him, and during the night he frequently did the same. Before the dawn he rose up to pray, in snow and frost and rain; nor was he overcome by tepidity, for his spirit was fervent within him. So the love of God and His fear increased more and more in his soul, and his faith grew strong, and his spirit was stirred within him with high and holy thoughts and aspirations.

It was not possible, that such a remarkable personality in a slave should escape notice. Milcho had three children and they seem to have been strongly attracted to the young herdsman. Throughout his life Patrick shared in his Divine Master's power of drawing the little ones irresistibly to him and winning their confidence. Milcho himself is said to have ordered Patrick to take charge of the education of his boy and two girls, a charge which the Saint used for the advantage of their souls by instructing them in the true faith. But this had to be done with much discretion, for Milcho was a druid, and, as such, was strongly opposed to the doctrines of Christianity which were at the time quietly making their way into Ireland from the continent and from Roman Britain.

One night Milcho was alarmed by a mysterious dream. He thought that Patrick came into his house, breathing flames from his mouth and nostrils, and with flames also issuing from his eyes and ears. The entire face of the Saint was like a bright fire which threatened to burn the house and which actually enveloped the three children and consumed them to ashes. Milcho alone was able to save himself from the flames.

In the morning Milcho sent for Patrick and related his dream, which he called upon the Saint to interpret. The holy youth, enlightened by God, replied that the flames represented his own faith in the Blessed Trinity with which he was all on fire and enlightened, and with which he hoped to inflame and enlighten others by his preaching. This preaching, however, would be fruitless for Milcho, who would obstinately refuse to receive the light of heavenly grace and who would die in the darkness of his infidelity. His son and daughters, on the contrary, would embrace the true faith and the Holy Spirit would by His divine fire burn out all sin and evil from their souls. Then, having served the Lord in justice and sanctity all the days of their lives, they would die a holy death; and their relics venerated all over Ireland would cure many diseases and infirmities. The dream, thus interpreted, came true; for Milcho refused to be converted; but his son embraced the faith and became a bishop, while—

> "Milcho's daughters twain to Christ were born
> In baptism, and each Emeria named:
> Like rose-trees in the garden of the Lord
> Grew they and flourished. Dying young, one grave
> Received them at Cluanbrain. Healing thence
> To many from their relics passed: to more
> The spirit's happier healing, Love and Faith."

The angel Victor, said to be the guardian of Ireland, held frequent communications with the future apostle. According to the pious chronicler, he sometimes appeared in human form, and at other times as a beautiful white bird. He taught Patrick "the right method of prayer, and watched over him and was a helper to him, a guardian in every danger, and a consolation after trouble." Kneeling upon the hillside or in the shadow of the woods, the holy youth would pray; and, when he rose up and went among men, he showed by his demeanour that he was filled with the grace of God. To fervent prayer he added fasting and practised many mortifications in addition to the ordinary trials of his servile state. All these he bore with patient resignation, thanking God for the graces which came with the trials, and acquiring thus early, doubtless, his life-long habit of receiving both pain and pleasure with a characteristic "Deo gratias."

Looking back upon these years of toil in bondage, the Saint recognised them as having been some of the most fruitful of his life, in regard to the progress of his soul in the paths of spirituality. In silence and solitude he laboured at his perfection, turning all things to his greater sanctification by patience, resignation and humble conformity to the Divine Will. Thus did he become, in the hands of God, a flexible instrument, a well- tempered sword, ready to fight the battles of the faith against the powers of darkness which still held full sway in Erin.

His spirit was not broken; it was only purified and strengthened in the furnace of affliction. Hope was still strong within him; not only the hope of attaining a better life after the exile of this world, but the strong hope given to the young that, however dark the present may appear, there are better days to come even here below. He prayed hard for the realisation of these earthly hopes that he might one day find freedom and see once more his country and his friends.

His desires and petitions were at last granted. He tells us that after six years of bondage he heard one night, while asleep, a voice saying to him:

"Thou dost fast well; soon shalt thou return to thy country."

And again after a short time the same voice said—

"Behold, thy ship is ready."

At the same moment he was enlightened as to the manner of his deliverance, and he understood that he would have a long journey to make in order to find the ship.

The prospect of once more seeing home, friends and country, filled the young captive's heart with intense joy. Confiding in the divine promise and inspired with indomitable courage he resolved to undertake all the risks connected with the accomplishment of his enterprise. Eluding the vigilance of his master, he set out at the first favourable opportunity, and under the divine guidance in the strength of God, who "prospered his way for good," he escaped all snares and the pursuit of Milcho's servants.

His route lay in the direction of the west coast, and probably towards the port which now bears the name of Killala. To reach this spot from Slemish he had to pass through the wood of Fochlut, where he met with some pleasant experiences of hospitality. The little children, as usual, treated him with kindness and confidence, and predisposed their parents in favour of the weary traveller. He was drawing successfully towards the close of his long journey of some two hundred miles, when he stopped for a night at the hut of a man called Gleru, who, with his good wife, gave food and lodging to Patrick. The two infant daughters of his host, "all light and laughter, angel-like of mien," were so attracted to the saintly youth that they never lost the hope of seeing him again, and their voices, "borne from the black wood o'er the midnight seas," were among those of the Irish children who always called him back. They waited for him faithfully, and he had at last, as we shall see, the happiness of baptizing them and receiving their vows of virginity.

His faith and confidence in God were severely tried when he reached the ship. It was about to sail, and the captain, not in the best of tempers, was unwilling to burden it further. When Patrick requested this man to take him on board, offering to work for his passage, he replied churlishly:

"You must on no account attempt to come with us."

Keenly disappointed, but nevertheless trusting in the power of God, the youth turned and prepared to seek once more the hospitable shelter of Gleru's roof. As he went he prayed, and soon he heard footsteps pursuing him and a breathless sailor shouting:

"Come quickly. These men are calling thee."

With a grateful heart he forthwith returned to the ship, and almost immediately the anchor was raised and they put out to sea. For three days they sailed, and at last they came to land, but on what coast we cannot say with certainty. The men were traders, and part of their cargo consisted of dogs—Irish dogs, especially the wolf-hound, being greatly prized in other countries. Their journey led them overland, and for nearly a month they travelled on foot, leading their dogs in leash.

In a thinly populated country there was little food to be obtained, and at last the troop were on the verge of starvation, many of the dogs falling exhausted by the way. In their dire extremity they turned to Patrick, who, though he had refused to ally himself closely with them because they were pagans, still treated them with charity in the hope that he might gain them to God. They admitted his ascendancy, obtained in much the same way as was the authority exercised by St Paul in a somewhat similar journey. He had not been silent on the way

St. Patrick called back by the Sailors.

with regard to the true God, and this was their opportunity for calling upon him to prove his assertions.

"Come now, O Christian!" said the captain, "thou sayest that thy God is great, all powerful, and merciful. Why, then, dost thou not pray to Him for us who are in danger of perishing for want of food? Ask Him to help us in our misery, that we may be delivered from death. For, according to all appearances, we shall never again behold the face of one of our fellow- creatures."

This was the occasion for which Patrick had been hoping and praying since he first joined company with them. Now was the moment for God to prove by a miracle to these ignorant and barbarous men that He was all good, powerful, and merciful, as the Saint had described Him. With firm confidence he replied:

"Turn earnestly with all your hearts to the Lord my God, to whom nothing is impossible. Believe fully and firmly in the God of heaven Who provides food for all His creatures, and I promise you that His liberality will give you in abundance all that you ask for. This very day your hunger shall be satisfied."

Saying this and similar things, Patrick raised their hopes and encouraged them to proceed on their way. Then praying fervently to that God, Who at the petition of Moses gave food to the Israelites in the desert, he found that his confidence was not in vain. For, by the help of God, it came to pass that a herd of swine crossed their path, and they were able to kill many of them. They remained in that place two nights, resting and refreshing themselves. The dogs also were provided for, a matter of great importance to the traders who had already lost some of them.

To complete their satisfaction they discovered a quantity of wild honey. And they gave sincere thanks to God for His mercy, and honoured Patrick so highly that one of them offered him some of the honey saying:—

"As a sacrifice do I offer thee this"—but the Saint with his usual "Deo gratias!" refused to accept it lest he should deprive God of some of the honour due to Him. And after that he partook no more of the honey.

As God permitted St Paul to be buffeted by an angel of Satan lest the greatness of his revelations should puff him up, so now after this miracle Patrick was tormented by the devil. The trial was of so terrible a nature that he could never lose the memory of it. As in the case of the first monk, St Anthony, or that of the Blessed Cure of Ars, nearer our own time, Satan was allowed to threaten the servant of God with corporal danger. A great rock appeared to fall upon him and he was unable to move his limbs.

He seemed to himself to be at the last extremity when it occurred to him to invoke the holy prophet Elias. "Elias, Elias!" he cried, and at that moment the sun rose in the heavens and the splendour of its beams enlightened him, while the heaviness that had oppressed him fell away and left him free. He adds in his "Confession":

"And I believe that Christ my Lord assisted me, and that His Spirit was even then crying out in my behalf. And I hope that it will be so in the day of my tribulation, as it is said in the Gospel 'On that day it is not you that speak but the Spirit of your Father that speaketh in you.' "

Being thus relieved and comforted Patrick rose and rejoined his companions, whom, to his great distress he found offering some of the flesh of the swine to their false gods. Fearlessly he upbraided them with their want of gratitude to the God Whom he had invoked in their favour and Who had mercifully succoured them in their need. Barbarous and heathen as they were, they listened to his words with respectful attention; and they were still further impressed when he refused to eat any more of the flesh, since it had been offered to idols, preferring to fast for the rest of the journey.

Nine days after the providential meeting with the swine, the party reached an inhabited region. Patrick soon found means of leaving the others quietly and without their knowledge; for he feared they would detain him, so greatly had they come to depend upon him. His great desire now was to make his way to his native place as quickly as possible; and though he tells us in his "Confession" that he was taken captive a second time, we have no means of deciding what effect this had upon his return.

Thus ended the period of severe probation which God had ordained for the greater perfection of His Apostle. From a human point of view it was disastrous to his whole career; but though Patrick himself deplores some of its effects, he did not look upon it from any standpoint but that of God's providence. "He was profoundly convinced," says Professor Bury, "that during the years of his bondage he had been held as in the hollow of God's hand; whatever hopes or ambitions he may have cherished in his boyhood must have been driven from his heart by the stress of his experience, and in such a frame of mind the instinct of a man of that age was to turn to a religious life."

A religious life meant study, and for this, as Patrick says himself, he had to some extent been rendered unfit; for "my speech and my style were changed into the tongue of the stranger, as can be easily seen in the quality of my writings." Nevertheless, during his six years of bondage he had been able to make acquaintance with the land of his future labours, to study the character of its inhabitants, and to learn their language in order that he might be able to accomplish a perfect work of conversion and secure the permanent foundation of his mission.

Chapter III

Monastic Training

T LAST, after years of exile and many months of weary travel, Patrick reached the home towards which his heart had always turned—the dear abode of his childhood, and the dwelling- place of those who loved him. Though his parents were dead, he was welcomed as a son by other relations, who strove by their warm affection and hospitable invitations to keep him in their midst. Gladly would he have remained, had not the higher call continued to sound importunately in his ears.

Like Abraham he had to leave country and home behind him, and go forth in search of the means ordained by God for the accomplishment of his mission. When all preparations were completed, he was once more to turn his steps towards the land of exile, not this time as an unwilling captive, but as the joyful messenger of good tidings to those who still sat in darkness and in the shadow of death. Like Joan of Arc in later days, he heard voices calling him to the great work that lay before him. The children of Ireland, of those and of future ages, sang ever in his mind their pitiful chant, "We beseech thee, holy youth, come once more and walk amongst us!"

Patrick says in his "Confession" that he had a supernatural experience similar to that of the great Apostle, St Paul, who, one night as he slept, saw a man of Macedonia, on whose lips were the words, "Pass over into Macedonia and help us." A certain Victoricus, whom he recognised as from Ireland, stood by Patrick's bedside holding many letters. One of these he selected and handed to the Saint, who read the title, "The Voice of the Irish," but, being overcome by emotion, could see no more. Then he heard voices speaking in the tongue of those who dwelt in Fochlut Wood, and the refrain was ever the same, beseeching him to come and bring them the good tidings of salvation. Those pleadings from the shore of the Western Sea touched him to the heart, and the Saint concludes his account of the vision with the words, "Thanks be to God that after very many years the Lord granted to them according to their earnest cry."

If any thought of settling down to a life of ease and comfort, in compliance with the wishes of his friends, had lingered in Patrick's mind, it was entirely dispelled by this vision. His vocation was now fully revealed to him, and nothing remained but to follow it out to the end, however sad the partings it entailed, however great the sacrifices it required. Still, so difficult an enterprise was not to be rashly undertaken, and doubts of the reality of his call may sometimes have assailed his mind. Many years afterwards, his "Confession" was written for the very purpose of showing that he had simply obeyed an irresistible call from God when he devoted himself to his mission.

"On another night," he says, "whether within me or beside me, I know not, in the clearest words, which I heard but could not understand, save at the end of the prayer, He spoke out thus:—'He who laid down His life for thee, He it is Who speaketh in thee.' And then I awoke filled with joy. And again another time I saw Him praying in me, as it were within my body, praying strongly with groanings."

"Then saw I—terrible that sight, yet sweet—
Within me saw a Man that in me prayed
With groans unutterable. That Man was girt
For mission far. My heart recalled that word,
'The Spirit helpeth our infirmities;
That which we lack we know not, but the Spirit
Himself for us doth intercession make,
With groanings which may never be revealed.'
That hour my vow was vowed, and He approved,
My Master and my guide."

God does not ask for impossibilities. When he sends a vocation, He provides all that is necessary to carry it out—the supernatural graces and the temporal opportunities, together with light, showing how to use both to the greatest advantage. It is man's fault if he falls short. But Patrick did not fall short. He had—

"Comforted on hills of Dalaraide,
His hungry heart with God, and, cleansed by pain
In exile found the Spirit's native land."

There his soul had been raised in prayer to heights of sublime contemplation; while his mind was filled with knowledge of the people he was to evangelize, and the language he was to use in communicating God's message to them. His practical common sense told him that this was much, yet not sufficient equipment for a successful mission.

He did not take the cry of the children to mean that he must set out at once, and risk life and freedom by throwing himself upon the mercy of his former masters. On the contrary, he distinguished the steps by which God intended him to advance, and he resolutely determined to take them. The first thing to be done was to repair as best he could the breach which his captivity had so rudely made in his education. As he thought the matter over, it seemed to him that nowhere could he find better guidance than under the care of his saintly relative, the great Martin, Bishop of Tours.

Of this holy prelate T. W. Allies writes:—

"He was in truth a man of mind, one of the most distinguished, the most amiable, and powerful bishops whom Gaul has ever produced, equally honoured by the great and powerful of the land, and by the people." But Martin was not merely a great bishop; he was also a devout monk. About two miles from Tours he had founded the famous monastery of Marmoutier, in a spot so quiet and secluded that he had but to retire there in order to find himself, as it were, in the solitude of a desert. Bounded on the one hand by a gentle curve in the river Loire, and on the other by inaccessible cliffs, the only approach was by a narrow path easily closed against intruders. Each monk dwelt in a separate cell, either built of wood, like that of St Martin himself, or hollowed out in the rock. They met in a common refectory for their single repast at sundown, and assembled in the church at the usual hours for divine service. No work was undertaken by them except that of writing, and this only by the younger monks. The elders occupied themselves with prayer alone.

It was with great reluctance that St Martin had accepted his appointment to the see of Tours. Far rather would he have hidden his life with Christ in God, in the dear solitude of a monastery, and even in the midst of the cares of his diocese he remained a monk at heart. He was now about eighty years of age, but time had not diminished the austerity of his life, nor weakened his influence over the souls of men.

Towards this school of sanctity Patrick directed his steps, accompanied by his angel who was to him as Raphael to the young Tobias. It was winter when he reached the Loire, and there was no means of crossing the swollen waters. But we are told that, full of confidence, the Saint cast his mantle on the surface of the stream, and, stepping upon it, was borne safely to the other bank. The picture is a beautiful one. The young man's hands are clasped in fervent prayer; the angel stands beside him with protecting wings outspread, while winds and waters, stilled for a moment, bear them gently on.

Another miracle presently occurred. The further bank of the river was bleak and desolate and the wayworn traveller was too weary to proceed on his journey. Darkness had closed in, so he cast himself on the ground beneath the frost-covered branches of a blackthorn tree, there to pass the night, as he had often had occasion to do, in the open air. But a heavenly warmth descended upon the tree, and, melting the frost, caused buds to swell and burst, as if the sunshine of springtime had come. In the morning the Saint found himself beneath a lovely canopy of full-blown blossoms, gleaming white in the mild surrounding air, while beyond, the country lay black and frozen. Each year, they say, the miracle is repeated in memory of the Apostle's passage, and anyone may see the wonderful blackthorn blossoms braving the frost and snow of late December, near the church and railway-station of "St Patrice."

Patrick was cordially welcomed at Marmoutier, where he at once entered upon a severe course of monastic training, without, however, binding himself to remain for life in the monastery. Hitherto he had served God in saintly fashion, it is true, but never had he found himself under strict discipline. Watching, prayer and fasting were familiar to him, but he had carried out these holy practices according to his own will and the divine inspirations with which he was favoured. He was wholly untrained in the virtue of religious obedience, and the observance of a fixed rule. Though, later, he became a past master in the art of bringing up young monks, his own early experiences were a source of trials and humiliations, which he used as illustrations of his teaching. The following story is said to have been told by him to show how needful it is for a monk to practise self-denial.

Meat was not allowed at Marmoutier, except in case of illness. Up to this time Patrick's fasting had restricted rather the quantity than the quality of his food, and he grew weary of continual abstinence. By some means he obtained a piece of meat, perhaps the portion of a sick brother who was unable to eat it. Fearing scandal, he hid his treasure in a jar, until he should find an opportunity of consuming it without being observed. Meanwhile, in going about his usual occupations, he came face to face with an extraordinary creature with eyes looking both forward and backward. The Saint, fearless, though astonished, asked what the apparition might be.

"I am a servant of God," answered the strange being; "with my ordinary eyes in front I see the ordinary actions of men, but with the eyes in the back of my head I saw a certain monk hiding a piece of meat in a jar, that he might escape observation."

With this the apparition vanished.

Thereupon Patrick prostrated himself on the ground, striking his breast with deep contrition and many tears, and solemnly promising never again in the whole course of his life to eat flesh meat—a promise which he faithfully kept. In response to his ardent prayers, the angel Victor, came to comfort him, and to tell him that his fault was forgiven. Patrick asked for a proof of his forgiveness, and was told to take the meat into the presence of the community, and there to cast it into water. Having thus publicly acknowledged his guilt, he was rewarded by seeing the meat changed into excellent fish. The half-humorous tone of this story does not prevent it from conveying a practical lesson.

Under St Martin's gentle care the deficiencies in Patrick's

education were attended to, and he advanced daily, not only in virtue but in learning. He was privileged to see the edifying death of the great and holy bishop, laid at his own request on the ground on sackcloth strewn with ashes, and surrounded by his weeping disciples. And, among the two thousand monks who attended St Martin's funeral, we may be sure that St Patrick was present, clad in his monastic habit of camel's hair, his head covered by the cowl which concealed the clerical tonsure given to him but lately by Martin himself.

From Tours, where he was no longer detained by his affection and reverence for its saintly bishop, Patrick moved on to the town of Auxerre, at that time the episcopal see of St Amator. As Amator was growing old he was anxious to find a successor who should carry on his work. He fixed upon the governor of the province, the young duke Germanus, whose sterling worth he had discovered under the appearance of a man of the world, wholly devoted to secular business and pleasure. In a dramatic scene, such as the people of those early ages dearly loved, Amator despoiled Germanus of his rich garments, costly ornaments, and weapons. He then clothed him in the habit of religion, telling him that God called him to leave the world, and to prepare to become his successor in the see of Auxerre. It must have been about this time that St Patrick reached the city, and was, according to some accounts, ordained deacon by St Amator, together with two of his future companions on the Irish mission. One of them, Iserninus, is said to have been of Irish nationality, and it appears that there was some connection between the Irish Christians and Auxerre. The other, Auxilius, is mentioned as one of the many nephews of St Patrick, who became clerics.

It is not impossible that Germanus should have joined these three in their studies, and that all four should have set out together to spend some time in the celebrated monastery

of Lerins, where we know that St Patrick lived for several
years at this period of his life. Lerins was just then rising into
prominence, and was soon to become the most renowned
school of learning and sanctity in the world. In that age of what
is called "the wandering of the nations," it was not easy to live in
peace on the mainland, where at any moment invading hordes
of barbarians might break in upon the quiet of the cloister.
Monasteries and convents, therefore, were often founded upon
islands, so that St Ambrose, speaking of the monastic life, says
of the coasts of Italy in his days:

"Why should I enumerate the islands which the sea wears
as a necklace? Here they who fly from the snares and vanities
of the world choose to lie hidden and unknown. Thus the sea
becomes a secure haven and an incentive to devotion, the sweet
chant of psalms blends with the gentle murmur of the waves,
and the islands lift up their voice of joy like a full chorus to the
hymns of their holy inhabitants."

Lerins was, up to the close of the fourth century, a desert
island, infested by snakes. It is one of a small group in the
Mediterranean, off the south-east coast of France, about
two miles from the present watering-place of Cannes. Here
St Honoratus, weary of the pomp and empty glitter of the
world, retired with a select body of companions to serve God
in solitude and prayer; while his sister, St Marguerite, took
possession of the larger island, nearer the mainland, where she
ruled over a community of fervent nuns.

The monks drove out the snakes, dug wells of sweet water
which flowed in gentle streams to the sea, and planted fair
trees, the shade of which tempered the summer heat. The
island became an earthly paradise, its rich verdure enamelled
with bright flowers and its forests sheltering innumerable
birds. Its products supplied every want of its pious inhabitants,
so that it was not long before the monks were able to devote

themselves almost exclusively to study and writing. So well did they apply themselves to their books that their monastery in a short time became a centre of all the knowledge and learning of the age. The broad, and even modern, views of its scholars are well expressed by St Vincent of Lerins, a contemporary of St Patrick:

"Let there be progress, therefore," he says, "a widespread and eager progress in every century and epoch, both of individuals and of the general body; of every Christian and of the whole Church; a progress in intelligence, knowledge and wisdom, but always within their natural limits, and without sacrifice of the identity of Catholic teaching, feeling, and opinion."

Vincent was one of the great glories of Lerins. Though we do not know what his influence over Patrick may have been, it was surely in itself an education to live near him. There was at this time another Saint residing in the monastery who was afterwards to be closely associated with St Patrick and St Germanus. This was Lupus, who became bishop of Troyes, celebrated for his heroic stand against Attila, King of the Huns, at the gates of his episcopal city.

"Who art thou?" demanded the intrepid bishop.

"I am Attila," replied the barbarian, "whom men call the Scourge of God."

St Lupus warned Attila that as the Scourge of God he might act only according to the Divine Will. His advice prevailed and the conqueror spared the city and its environs, though he kept the Saint as a hostage for a considerable time. Well it was for Patrick to be associated with such men as these during the years of his training for his own episcopate. The death of St Amator in the year 418 caused Germanus to be hastily consecrated Bishop of Auxerre, but his previous education had been so thorough, and his talents were so unmistakable, that he needed but little preparation. He had studied for the law in

Rome, with brilliant success, his natural gifts being cultivated to the highest degree of polished elegance. As a bishop he lived a life of apostolic simplicity, but he brought the treasure of his talents and his wide experience into the service of his diocese and of the Church.

At Lerins, Patrick attained an intimate acquaintance with the monastic life, its needs, its methods and its standard of perfection. We shall see how fully he benefited by this branch of his studies, when, in the course of his apostolic labours, we find him founding monasteries and convents for the youths and maidens of Ireland who came to him in crowds to beg admission to the religious life. No examples could have been better than those provided by Providence for his edification in the persons of St Martin, St Germanus, St Honoratus, St Lupus, St Vincent of Lerins and the multitude of holy monks and nuns who in this and the neighbouring island had consecrated their lives to God.

After years spent at Lerins, and perhaps also some stay in the monastery of Arles, St Patrick seems to have rejoined St Germanus at Auxerre. The Pelagian heresy was at this time ravaging the British Church, whose bishops begged those of Gaul to come to their aid. With the approval of the Pope, St Germanus of Auxerre and St Lupus of Troyes were deputed to go to Britain and endeavour to root out the heresy. In all probability Patrick went with them. In the train of the bishops was also Palladius the deacon, who after a time seems to have been sent to Rome to report on the success of the mission. He carried with him a request from the few scattered Christians in Ireland for recognition as a church by the Holy See and for missionaries to preach the faith to their pagan countrymen. It thus came about that St Palladius received a commission from the Holy Father to preach to the Irish.

Meanwhile, in spite of the preference given to Palladius,

Patrick continued to hear the cry of the children from Fochlut Wood:

"All we Irish beseech thee, holy Patrick, to come and walk among us and to free us!" And again, "O holy Patrick, save us from the wrath to come!" And then the old refrain—

"We beseech thee, holy youth, come once more and walk amongst us!"

Thus continually urged by his voices, Patrick knew not what course to pursue. The angel Victor, protector of Ireland, at last spoke to him definitely, saying:

"Go to Ireland, for thou shalt be the Apostle of its people."

So Patrick determined to go to Rome and lay his case before the Pope. In the words of the poet, he says:

"Forthwith to Rome I fled; there knelt I down
Above the bones of Peter and of Paul,
And saw the mitred embassies from far,
And saw Celestine with his head high held,
Chief Shepherd of the Saviour's flock on earth,
Tall was the man, and swift; white-haired; with eye
Starlike and voice a trumpet-note that pealed
God's Benediction o'er the city and globe."

Chapter IV

The Work Begun

AFTER his return from his successful mission against Pelagianism, St Germanus naturally watched with the greatest interest the progress of Christianity in the British Isles. It was, therefore with deep concern that he learnt the ill-success attending the labours of St Palladius in Ireland. Want of knowledge of the language and character of the inhabitants, combined with failing health, prevented Palladius from advancing into the country; so that the spread of the gospel was limited to the few scattered Christian communities already existing and to three small new foundations.

The call of Patrick was not unknown to Germanus, and, in the present circumstances, his resolution to go to Rome met with the entire approval of the Bishop of Auxerre. In order that Patrick might be duly accredited, Germanus sent with him his most trusted and venerable priest, Segetius, bearing letters of introduction and recommendation to the Pope, St Celestine I, then gloriously reigning. They travelled, in all probability, by sea from some port in southern Gaul to Rome.

One account of their journey runs as follows:

"Now when Patrick had completed his sixtieth year and had learned the lore, unto him went his guardian angel, Victor, for he had been Patrick's helper when he abode in bondage to Milcho, and had helped him concerning everything he would desire. And Victor said to him: "Thou art commanded by God to go to Ireland, to strengthen faith and belief, and that thou mayest bring the Irish by the net of the gospel to the harbour of life. For all the Irish cry that so it must be; they think thy coming timely and mature.'

"Patrick then bade farewell to Germanus, and Germanus gave him a blessing; and a trustworthy old man went with him from Germanus, to guard him and testify for him. Segetius was his name, and a priest he was in rank, and at the ordinances of the Church he used to be at Germanus' hand. Then Patrick went to sea"—and coasting along the Mediterranean he met with a strange adventure and obtained the wonderful Staff of Jesus, so famous in his after career. The story goes on:

"It is then that he came to the island, and he saw the new house and the married couple in youth therein, and the withered old woman before the house.

" 'What is she?' asked Patrick; 'great is her feebleness.'

" 'She is a grand-daughter of mine,' replied the young man. "If thou wert to see her mother she is still more feeble.'

" 'How came that to pass?' asked Patrick.

" 'Not hard to say,' said the young man. 'We are here since the time of Christ, who came unto us when He dwelt among men, and we made a feast for Him. He blessed our house, and blessed ourselves, but that blessing came not upon our children; we, however, shall abide here, without age, without decay, until the Judgment. And it is long since thy coming was foretold unto us, for God left word with us that thou wouldst come to preach to the Gael, and He left a token with us, namely His Staff, to be given to thee.'

" 'I will not take it,' said Patrick, 'till He Himself gives me His Staff.'

"Patrick stayed there with them three days and three nights, and afterwards went to Mount Hermon in the neighbourhood of the island. And there the Lord appeared to him, and told him to go and preach to the Gael, and gave him the Staff of Jesus, and said that it would be a helper to him in every danger and in every unequal conflict in which he should be. And Patrick asked three boons of Him, namely, to be on His right hand in the kingdom of heaven; that he (Patrick) might be judge of the Gael on doomsday; and as much gold and silver as his nine companions could carry to be given to the Gael for believing."

Such is the legend, which has, nevertheless, a symbolical meaning. The facts commemorated by it are the pre-ordained mission of Patrick, and the supernatural assistance with which he was to be favoured during its course. His Master, Jesus, was sending him upon his journey and from Jesus alone would Patrick expect help and strength in all his labours. That this mighty staff did not fail him in his need will be amply proved by the sequel of this narrative.

Pope Celestine received Patrick favourably, listened to his account of his mystical call to convert Ireland, and finally dismissed him with the necessary authorisation to take up the task of Palladius should it be proved that he had withdrawn from it. The party then set out on their return journey towards Auxerre.

On the way they were met by messengers with the news of the death of Palladius, and nothing now prevented Patrick from being consecrated bishop as a preliminary to his setting forth for Ireland. It is not certain where or by whom the ceremony of his consecration was performed. We are told, however, that on the same day Auxilius was ordained and Iserninus and others of Patrick's household. "And while the consecration was going on, the three choirs responded to each other; namely, the choir of the household of heaven, and the choir of the Roman clerics, and the choir of the children from the wood of Fochlut. This is what all sang: 'All we Irish beseech thee, holy Patrick, to come and walk among us and to free us.' "

It was, indeed, time that the faith of Christ should be preached to the Irish. The Gospel had already spread over the greater part of the Roman Empire, and there was no reason why the beautiful island in the far west should remain in darkness. "Ireland," says St Bede, "for wholesomeness and serenity of climate, far surpasses Britain. It is a land flowing with milk and honey, nor is it wanting in vines, fish, or fowl, and it is remarkable for deer and goats." Flocks and herds found ample pasture on its rich meadows; swarms of bees made their hives in its thick forests and gathered honey from the luxuriant growth of its flowers. Its oak-trees provided acorns for the large herds of swine kept in the glades of its forests, the timber of which was used for ships employed in war or in traffic with Britain and the continent.

The sea-coast of Ireland by its irregularity formed magnificent natural harbours in which the fleets of the world might safely ride at anchor. In the interior the undulating surface, rising here and there into lovely hills and mountain ranges, was diversified by noble rivers and exquisite lakes. Beneath the emerald verdure, kept constantly fresh by the abundance of waters, there lay hid treasures of gold, silver, iron and other metals to be obtained for the labour of mining. Rare marbles and precious stones came from its quarries, while mussel pearls of large size and great beauty were plentiful in its rivers. These advantages of nature were utilised by the skill of the inhabitants who had attained to great perfection in some of the arts, particularly in that of metal work and ornamentation.

The people were simple, brave, warm-hearted, loyal, and deeply religious according to their lights. No taint of the widespread corruption of the times had reached them, for no conquering Roman had ever set foot upon the soil of this privileged spot of earth. An elaborate system of government prevailed, and all persons were subject to the minute control of the Brehon laws. The Ard-ri, or High King, ruled in Tara over his sub-kings, who, in their turn, had petty kings beneath them. The tribal system fostered union between people and rulers, though it did not prevent the frequent clash of war between rival chieftains.

The native tongue was very rich and perfect, and had an oral literature of its own. Poetry and music were industriously cultivated; the harp resounded in the royal halls of Tara, and the immemorial bagpipe roused the warlike ardour of the troops as they marched to battle. Christianity was not unknown. To other nations it had been brought by the Christian soldiers of invading armies; to Ireland it first came from ever-friendly Spain.

In order to avoid the hostile Roman ships, Irish trading vessels crossed direct from their own island to the Spanish coast, and thence transacted their business with the other countries of Europe. Thus it was that they came into contact with the new religion which was changing the face of the heathen Roman Empire. But the Irish Christians, few and scattered as they were, felt the need of organisation, and it was chiefly for this that St Palladius had come among them. The mission of St Patrick, on the contrary, was a determined and successful effort to convert the whole island to the faith of Christ and to unite it inseparably to the See of Rome.

Invested with full powers, and supplied with every requisite, including a numerous suite of saintly and learned men, Patrick set sail for the goal of his highest and holiest aspirations. He was mature in years, inured to hardship and privations, dauntless in courage, cheerful in disposition; and, though meek and humble of heart, prepared to defend God's cause in the presence of heathen kings and their attendant magicians.

It was the year of Our Lord 432. Had Patrick set out earlier he would have lacked his best experience; later, he would have lost his best years. God had foreseen all, provided for all, and now He sent his finished instrument to do His work, and to light that flame of faith, which was to illumine the West from its first kindling to the day of doom.

But however imposing his personality, and however weighty his knowledge and experience, he required material support to enable him to make his way against the obstacles which would surely beset his path. This had been amply supplied from the flourishing Church of Gaul. Nor was the friendly succour of Rome lacking—that mother and mistress of all the churches, whose maternal care stretched then, as now, from end to end of the known world, in obedience to the command of the Divine Master: "Going, therefore, teach ye all nations, baptizing them in the name of the Father, and of the Son, and of the Holy Ghost. Teaching them to observe all things, whatsoever I have commanded you; and behold, I am with you all days, even to the consummation of the world."

Our Saint was now a bishop and a direct successor of the Apostles, endowed with the plenitude of Orders, and authorised by his mission from the Holy See to preach the faith to the men of Ireland. He carried with him in his ship most precious relics, but precious above all were those of the holy Apostles St Peter and St Paul. He had abundance of priestly vestments and sacred vessels for the service of the altar, together with the necessary books for the divine office. Besides these, his ship contained such treasures as would by their display attract the attention and respect of the people, while inclining them to give greater credit to the words spoken by the missionaries.

After a prosperous voyage—we are not told from what port—the Wicklow Hills, "the holy hills of Ireland," came in sight. The voyagers sailed along the eastern coast seeking a suitable landing place, until they reached the low beach of Inver Dea, the mouth of the Dee, now the river Vartry. Here they disembarked, and seeing some fishermen drawing in their nets they asked to be allowed to purchase fish. Their reasonable request was refused, and Patrick, grieved that his hungry and dispirited followers should be thus inconvenienced, foretold that henceforth the river would produce no fish.

But Patrick was not to be repelled by a few fishermen. He understood the people well, and from his first arrival in the country he made it his invariable custom to present himself in person to the chieftain of the district he proposed to visit. The party pushed on, therefore, towards the fortress of Nathi, son of Garrchon, a churlish man, who had already shown small courtesy to St Palladius on his landing at the same place. Nathi, on being informed of Patrick's approach, assembled his followers and drove the missionaries from his territory. For this ungracious act they were punished by an inroad of the sea which turned that portion of their land into a salt marsh, utterly useless and unproductive.

Still, this first attempt was not wholly unsuccessful, for Sinell, son of Finchad, was here the first man in Ireland who believed in God through Patrick's preaching. Patrick blessed him and his descendants, and left with him his deacon, Mantan, to instruct the new disciples and any other men of goodwill who might accept the faith. It was here that Mantan (the toothless) gained his name, his front teeth being broken by a blow from a stone in the affray. Possibly the deacon was not in a fit condition to continue the journey, and Sinell may have shown him kindly attention and offered him hospitality.

This rebuff determined Patrick to re-embark and press northward to that part of the country which he knew, where he was known, and, by some, beloved. Although Milcho had been a hard taskmaster, his children had won the affection of the young slave, who had found means to give them some instruction in the Christian religion. Their voices, no doubt, were among those that called him, and he yearned to preach the faith to their elders also. Among his fellow-servants he must have made friends upon whose support he could now rely.

"It seemed fitting to him, since he had at first done service to Milcho's body that now he should do service to his soul. So he showed his mast to land and went prosperously voyaging along the eastern coast of Ireland, till he anchored at Inver Domnann." They hoped to find fish there but were disappointed; and, as night had fallen, they remained until dawn. A little farther on they came to three rocky islets, one of which is now called Inis-Patrick. Here, however, there was nothing to be had, so Patrick sent a boat to the mainland to seek for food. The messengers found none, and things were beginning to look serious, for the company on board was large and important.

At length, however, they were hospitably received at the house of a man called Sescnen, father of the gentle boy Benen, or Benignus, so dearly loved by Patrick later on. The famished guests were fed and cared for; then, wearied with travel and ceaseless toil, they lay down upon the grass to rest, and Patrick slept. Little Benen had already made friends with Patrick, and now he stood rapt as it were in ecstasy and gazed upon the Saint. With his innocent eyes he saw, perchance, what others could but dimly guess at: the beauty of the Apostle's soul, all bent upon God's glory and the good of men. Never was there a sweeter child than Benen, nor one more tactful and delicate in his attentions to those he loved and revered. Suddenly bethinking himself, he ran and gathered all the sweet-smelling flowers he could find, and, returning, he placed them gently in Patrick's bosom. But the men of Patrick's household reproved him, saying that he would awake their master. Patrick heard their words and said, "Let the boy alone, for he shall be the heir of my kingdom," meaning that Benignus would become coadjutor bishop of Armagh, with a right of succession to the see. But Benignus was destined to die before Patrick, and the succession went to another.

So strong was the attraction of Benignus for the blessed Patrick that he could not be separated from him. Sescnen provided a chariot to convey the Saint on his journey, and at the moment of departure, when Patrick had one foot in the chariot, the boy seized the other and cried out that he must go with his father, Patrick. Then the Saint told one of his clerics to baptize the child, and he took him with him as his first Irish disciple, instructing him, and having him taught all that a young cleric should know. Benignus proved a treasure of sanctity, learning and wisdom, and was particularly remarkable for his beautiful voice and for his skill in ecclesiastical music. His gentle and happy disposition endeared him not only to Patrick but to all who knew him. We shall hear more of him later.

The tender devotion of the people of Ireland to the Blessed Mother of God owes its origin to the seeds planted by St Patrick. He always honoured her himself with great devotion, and he could never endure that anyone should fail in respect towards her. He was soon to have an opportunity of proving his loyalty to his Queen. While journeying and preaching in these parts, he met with a certain wizard who had the temerity to mock at his words when he spoke of the virginity of Mary. Struck with horror at the blasphemy, Patrick made the sign of the cross upon the earth, which forthwith opened and swallowed up the wicked man in the sight of the assembled multitude.

This was the first and last occasion on which Patrick found such severity necessary. Devotion to Our Blessed Lady seemed to spring up naturally on Irish soil, and, though we hear but little of it from the chroniclers, we know that the greater number of the earliest churches were dedicated to Mary, Queen of Virgins.

IRABILIS
Deus in sanctis suis. Spi-
ritus Sanctus, à quo omne
donum, et gratiarum charis-
mata utrique, et novi et ve-
teris Testamenti Ecclesiæ, da-
ta, hæc protulit per os Regii
Psalmistæ Davidis filii, &c.

St. Patrick Blessing Ireland.

Having reached the coast, the missionaries found their boat and once more embarked. Voyaging northwards in sight of land, they came to Inver Slan, where the thick foliage invited them to go on shore and provided a safe hiding place for the boat. They then sought a retired spot where they might rest and refresh themselves both spiritually and corporally. But a swineherd had noticed the suspicious action of hiding the boat, and, without inquiring their business or seeking to know the truth, he ran quickly and told his master, Dichu, that robbers were lurking in his land.

Dichu came at once to the spot, and, perceiving that there was some foundation for the swineherd's story, he set his dog at the strangers. The unarmed clerics had no protection but in Providence against the onslaught of the fierce Irish wolfhound. Patrick, with his wonted courage and trust in God, arose and faced the furious animal, chanting that verse of the inspired prophet:—

"Deliver not up to beasts, O Lord, the souls of them that confess to Thee."

Instantly, the baying hound held its peace and refused to attack the servants of God.

Dichu by this time had observed the peaceful aspect and dignified bearing of the holy company, and perceived that his own judgment, like that of his swineherd, had been too hasty. Grief of heart seized him at the thought of the injustice he had been about to commit. He greeted the strangers respectfully, and declared himself ready to listen to their teaching. Patrick was not slow to follow up the advantage thus offered to him. He explained the doctrines of the faith; Dichu believed and Patrick baptized him. "So that he is the first who received in Ulster baptism and belief from Patrick."

There stood near by a barn destined to become famous in Ireland, for upon its site the first Christian church was to be erected, and there, when his time came, Patrick was to die. Dichu offered the barn to the Saint, who said:—

> "God's blessing on Dichu,
> Who gave me the Barn!
> May he have afterwards
> A heavenly home, bright, pure, great!
> God's blessing on Dichu—
> On Dichu and his children!
> No child of his, nor grandchild,
> Whose life shall not be long!"

In memory of the gift, the place was called in Irish, Saball, or the Barn, a name which later became Saul. Here St Patrick and his companions remained for some time, building their first church and instructing their converts. Having now a foothold in Ireland, it was not necessary to return to the boat, of which the travellers were so weary. The journey could easily be made from Inver Slan to Slemish, and Patrick ardently desired to revisit the scene of his captivity. As soon as possible, therefore, he set out on foot, accompanied by a few of his attendants, and took the direct route for the home of his former master.

But Milcho had already heard of the approach of the missionaries. His hard old pagan heart could not brook the thought of listening to their preaching; nor could he, a druid, reconcile himself to the idea of facing a man who had once been his bond-servant, and who now returned to stand against him, backed by the might of imperial Rome, joined to the supernatural assistance of signs and miracles.

Doubtless, he mistook the nature of Patrick's mission. Had he waited to hear his words and to see the presents brought to him, he might have fared better. Milcho acted hastily, and brought upon himself the ruin of which he had dreamt in years gone by. Of the manner in which he perished, we read:—

"Now when Milcho heard that Patrick had arrived, he was not willing to believe and to quit the bad heathen law in which he was biding. He deemed it a shame to believe in his slave and to be subject to him. This is the counsel which the devil taught him. He entered his palace along with his gold and his silver, and he himself set fire to it and burnt it with the whole of his treasures; and his soul went to hell.

"Then Patrick stood still upon the southern side of Slemish—there stands a cross in that place—and he saw the fire from afar. He was silent for the space of two or three hours. At last, in the midst of sighs and groans, he said:—

"'Yonder is the fire of Milcho's house, for he hath burnt himself amidst his house, lest he should believe in God at the end of his life. He on whom the ban is lying, of him shall be neither king nor crown-prince, and in bondage shall his offspring and his seed abide for ever, and his soul shall not come out of hell up to doom nor after doom.' "

Terrible words, but words spoken in sorrow rather than in anger. Great as was Patrick's personal disappointment at this signal failure almost at the outset of his mission, he was still more grieved to think of the fate of the unhappy man's soul. But Milcho had no excuse for his conduct. Not in ignorance nor in blindness did he turn away from the light of the gospel, but in full knowledge, and with all the advantages of early lessons in the faith which now in his old age he wilfully rejected. The awful example was necessary, and Patrick did not shrink from pronouncing the words which were to convey the truth of eternal punishment to the minds of his hearers.

The Saint's northward journey terminated at Slemish, "and when he had spoken these words, he turned right-hand wise, and went back again into Ulster, until he came to Mag Inis, to Dichu, son of Grichem; and there he stayed a long while, sowing belief, until he brought all the Ulster men by the net of the Gospel to the harbour of life." This must mean all the Ulster men with whom he came in contact at the time, for the complete conversion of the province took place later.

Dichu had a brother, an old man named Ross, who dwelt in Durlus, to the south of Downpatrick, where the town of Bright now stands. It was natural that Patrick should wish to convert the brother of his benefactor. He went, therefore, to preach to him, but Ross refused to hear him, and "fought against him." Patrick reproached him with his neglect of preparation for the life to come, especially as, at his great age, there was no hope of enjoying the good things of this world. His arguments prevailed with Ross so far that he professed himself willing to believe with all his heart in anyone who should make him young again.

Thereupon, says the chronicler, Patrick prayed, and youth was restored to Ross, so that he became as handsome, brave and strong, as in his early years. He believed and was baptized, together with many others converted by the same miracle. Then Patrick asked him whether he would prefer to live his life over again or go at once to heaven. Ross wisely chose the immediate enjoyment of eternal life in heaven, and, having received Holy Viaticum, he died a peaceful and happy death.

St Patrick appointed Loarn, one of his disciples, bishop of Bright. We are told that Loarn had the courage to rebuke his master for hastiness on the following occasion. A little boy was playing with a hoop outside the church, and the noise he made disturbed the people at their devotions. Patrick, who was usually all affection and indulgence towards children, gave way to a moment's irritation, and seizing the boy by the arm, sternly ordered him to go away. Loarn respectfully reminded the Saint of Our Lord's words:—"Suffer the little children to come unto Me, and forbid them not, for of such is the Kingdom of Heaven," indicating that, by his severity, he had failed to observe this precept.

While St Patrick was journeying, he caught sight of a tender youth, Mochae by name, herding swine. Thoughts of his own occupation in the days of his bondage crowded upon him, and none knew better than he the possibilities of such a life for the contemplation of divine things. With the instinct of sanctity he understood that this innocent boy possessed faculties far above what his menial tasks required, and that of him it would be easy to make a fitting instrument for the spread of the faith. He had him carefully instructed, baptized him, and, later on, gave him the clerical tonsure and all things necessary for divine service, including a gospel and a credence table. He not only ordained Mochae priest, but when the time came for consecrating him bishop he bestowed upon him a crozier which he had received from heaven. "And because this crozier had fallen from heaven with its head in Patrick's bosom and its foot in Mochae's bosom, it was known as the winged crozier." If, as some writers say, Mochae was the grandson of Milcho, being the son of a daughter of Milcho, called Bronach, this was a further reason for his choice of the youth, and his kindness to him.

Such, as far as we can tell, were the beginnings of Patrick's labours in the land of his adoption. The promise of his early years had not been in vain; his long and arduous preparation was now about to produce a plentiful harvest, and God was visibly blessing his work. The incidents above related, often in the words of a literal translation of the original Irish, and with all their imaginative setting, show dimly how great was our Saint's zeal for the glory of God, and the salvation of souls. Like Our Lord Himself, he went about doing good, letting no opportunity escape of preaching the gospel to the poor and the ignorant, as well as to the worldly and the hard-hearted. Seldom did the good seed fall upon stony ground. The hearts of the men of Ireland were as that good soil where the seed springs up and bears fruit a hundred-fold.

Chapter V

The Great Contest at Tara

PATRICK spent the winter in works small and unimportant compared with the great design which led him towards Tara "as the high tide of Easter drew nigh." It seemed to him that there was no place fitter for the celebration of the most impressive solemnity of the year than Mag Breg, "the Beautiful Plain," then the "chief abode of the idolatry and wizardry of Ireland." God had ordained that the minds of the heathen should be deeply stirred by this first public appearance of the great Apostle.

Who has not heard of the hill of Tara and of its immemorial associations? There the High Kings of Erin held their court with all the pomp and magnificence at their disposal, and there at certain seasons they gathered round them their nobles, poets, bards and druids to give lavish entertainment to the sub-kings who came as their guests. On Holy Saturday A.D. 433, a solemn festival was to begin and in the evening bonfires were to be lighted. But until the sacred flame was seen to burn on Tara's hill all fires were strictly prohibited.

The reigning monarch at the time was Laeghaire (Leary)

son of the renowned Niall of the Nine Hostages, of whom we have already spoken. Laeghaire was not equal to his father in character or ability, but he was anxious to hold the sceptre in as firm a grasp, and not to lose power over the dependent kings. For this end he surrounded himself with all the learned druids and skilful magicians he could find. But these were the professed enemies of Christianity, and as Professor Bury says, "it must have been difficult for him to withstand the influence of the druids, who naturally put forth all their efforts to check the advance of the dangerous doctrine which had come from overseas to destroy their profession, their religion, and their gods."

Lochru and Lucat-Mael were his chief wizards, and, being false prophets, they foretold that "an evil teacher would come over the sea to their land; that a multitude would receive him, and that he would find love and reverence from the men of Ireland. Moreover, he would cast out from their realms the kings and lords, and would destroy all the idols; and the worship established by him would abide in the land for ever and ever." No doubt these druids had been informed of the progress of Christianity in Britain and throughout Europe. Their brethren abroad had been discredited, and they feared the same fate for themselves. It required no great spirit of prophecy to give the following description of a Christian missionary—a description taken by the ignorant for a personal portrait of Patrick. Two or three years before his arrival the lines were already current:

> "Adzehead will come over the raging sea,
> His mantle head-holed, his staff crook-headed,
> His table in the east of his house.
> All his household shall answer, Amen, Amen,
> Adzeheads will come who will build cities,
> Who will consecrate churches, pinnacled music-houses,
> Many conical caps, a realm round croziers."

The adzehead was the tonsured cleric; the head-holed mantle was the chasuble; the crook-headed staff, the crozier;

the table in the east of his house, the altar at the east end of the church or music-house surmounted by the conical cap of the belfry. These were, according to the druids, the fatal signs of the destruction of heathenism and idolatry, and with them their own influence and authority. And as it was prophesied and prefigured so, indeed, it came to pass. No wonder the wizards exerted all their arts and magic powers to keep at bay this their deadly enemy; no wonder Patrick had an all-important battle to fight for the truth.

The time had come for the great trial of arms between the ancient forces of druidism and the religion which, though new to the pagans, yet dated back to the beginning of time. Leaving the friendly hospitality of Dichu and bidding him a grateful farewell, the holy company put their vessel to sea and went southwards till they anchored at Inver Colptha, the mouth of the river Boyne. There Patrick left his boat in charge of his nephew, Lomman, who was to rejoin him quietly in a few days. The missionaries followed the course of the stream for about twelve miles until they came to the hill of Slane, where Patrick proposed to spend the Easter festival.

While they rested on the summit of this lofty height their eyes beheld a magnificent view on every side. Flowing beneath them was the river Boyne, its fertile banks clothed with the delicate verdure of early spring; to the north, far away in the distance clothed with purple mist, rose the mountains of Mourne which they had lately left; and to the south lay the beautiful hills of Wicklow. Against this background stood boldly out, ten miles away, but seeming much nearer, the royal hill of Tara, the roofs of its palaces gilded by the last rays of the setting sun. The theatre was a fitting one for the enaction of the great drama which was to end in the tragic passing of heathenism and the triumphal entrance of the Gospel of Christ.

Such it certainly appeared to those who were the first to

frame the story in its poetic setting. "The bitter hostility of the druids and the relations of Laeghaire to Patrick" says Professor Bury, "were worked up by Irish imagination into a legend which ushers in the Saint upon the scene of his labours with great spectacular effect. The bold and brilliant idea of the first Easter fire flashing defiance across the plain of Meath to the heathen powers of Tara, and the vision of the King with his Queen and sorcerers setting forth from their palace in the depth of night with chariots arid horses, and careering over the plain, as Ailill and Maeve of pagan story might have suddenly driven in headlong course against the Hound of Ulaid, is a picture not unworthy of the best of those nameless story-makers who in all lands, working one cannot tell where, or how, transfigure the facts of history. Bearing this in mind we shall proceed with our narrative.

When the sun had sunk in the west and darkness enshrouded the land, Patrick prepared to perform the opening ceremony of the blessed night preceding the celebration of the Resurrection of Christ. A truly blessed night it was for Ireland and her children, when for the first time the paschal fire was kindled, never more to be extinguished in the land. Then, as now, it was new fire, produced by the contact of flint and steel, and sanctified by some of the most beautiful prayers in the liturgy of the Church. The "Lumen Christi" flamed forth and Heaven and earth joined in a triumphant "Deo gratias!"

Hardly were the Christian torches seen to blaze when the attention of the High King was drawn to the prodigy. The whole of Mag Breg, the Beautiful Plain, was illuminated, while Tara yet remained in darkness. Angrily the monarch called his attendants and bade them go and inquire who had thus dared to break the law made by himself for the occasion.

The druids were, doubtless, well aware of all the movements of Patrick, and it may have been at their instigation that

Laeghaire made the particular law which only held good in general for the two great festivals of Beltane and Samhain. All their powers must now be put forth in order to ward off the threatened destruction. They told Laeghaire that there was no need to send messengers as far as Slane to ask what the fire meant, for—

"We see the fire," they said, "and we know that, unless it is quenched on the night on which it was made, it will not be quenched till doomsday. He, moreover, who kindled it, will vanquish the kings and lords of Ireland, unless he is forbidden."

"This shall not be!" cried the king, "but we will go and slay the man who kindled the fire."

There was great bustle and hurrying to and fro on the hill of Tara, stamping of horses and shouting of men, while chariots were being yoked for the midnight excursion. On Slane, in the meantime, the peaceful office was sung and all the ceremonies of Easter Eve were decorously carried out by Patrick and his household. The camp of Christ and the camp of Satan were drawn up in deadly rivalry; demons hovered darkly over Tara, while the calm legions of the angelic host kept guard over Slane. Patrick, with the Staff of Jesus for his standard, and with Victor, the guardian spirit of Ireland by his side, had no need to fear for the result of the contest.

It was late in the night when nine chariots fared forth, bearing the king and queen, the two chief wizards, and a number of the nobles. The horses galloped swiftly over the plain, followed, no doubt, by a crowd of people eager to see the end of the affair, though of such persons the story does not speak.

Soon the wizards began to fear lest by too hasty action the monarch might fail in his object. Driving up within speaking distance of the royal chariot:

"Thou shouldst take heed," they cautioned the king, "not to go to the place where the fire was made, that thou mayest not thereby do reverence to the man who kindled it. Rather stay outside, and let him be called out to thee, that he may judge that thou art the King and that he is the subject; and we will argue in thy presence."

"That is good advice," answered the king, well pleased by their flattery, "it shall be done as you say."

They drove to the place called "The Graves of Fiacc's Men," and there they unyoked the horses from the chariots. The king and his nobles sat them down in solemn state, the warriors with their shields erect in front of them. And every man rested his chin upon the rim of his shield, looking grim and terrible in the light of the flaring torches. We may suppose that the queen with her attendants remained in the shelter of her chariot. It was ordained that no one should rise to show respect to the strangers, though a command so contrary to the native ideas of courtesy seems to have been given and obeyed with reluctance.

All being in readiness a messenger was sent to bid Patrick come forth and appear in the royal presence. Soon a bright procession was seen descending the hill, the sacerdotal vestments of the clerics gleaming in the torchlight. As Patrick advanced, with his crozier, the Staff of Jesus in his hand, all eyes were fixed upon him. Calmly and with great dignity he chanted as he approached the royal party, that most appropriate verse of the nineteenth psalm:

"Some trust in chariots and some in horses: but we will call upon the name of the Lord our God."

As the Saint's clear strong voice resounded through the night a feeling of awe and reverence filled the minds of all, so that in spite of themselves the warriors could hardly keep their position, seated as they were, their chins upon their shields. One man, indeed, Erc, the son of Deg, "in whom was a nature from God," rose to his feet to greet St Patrick. Vanquished in a moment by grace, he believed in God; and Patrick bestowed a fervent blessing upon him. Later on he was baptized and became the first bishop of Slane. And Patrick said to him, "Thy city on earth shall be high and noble," and his relics were afterwards venerated in Slane.

After a short dialogue between Patrick and Laeghaire in which "each asked tidings of the other," apparently on terms of equality, the wizard Lochru attacked the Saint "angrily and noisily and with contention and questions." Not satisfied with malicious insinuations he be came openly hostile and violent, daring even to blaspheme the mystery of the Blessed Trinity, and the other truths of the Catholic Faith. Small wonder was it that Patrick's anger was roused, and that looking wrathfully upon the impious wizard he exclaimed, with a loud voice calling upon God—

"O Lord, Who canst do all things, and on Whose power dependeth all that exists, Thou Who hast sent us hither to preach Thy name to the heathen, let this ungodly man, who blasphemeth Thy name, be lifted up and let him forthwith die!"

The miracle was at once accomplished in the sight of the wondering multitude. No sooner had the words been uttered than a supernatural force raised the unhappy wizard into the air, whence he fell heavily down, his head striking upon a stone, so that he died in the presence of the assembly. Thereupon the heathen were so impressed that their opposition was subdued, seeing that Patrick was more powerful than their druids.

But King Laeghaire was enraged at the fate of Lochru, on whom he had greatly depended in all his difficulties. In revenge he wished to take the life of Patrick.

"Slay the cleric!" he cried to his guards.

But the Saint stood firmly at his post holding the Staff of Jesus in his hand. With flashing eyes and resonant voice he sang the verse—

"Let God arise and let His enemies be scattered: and let them that hate Him flee from before His face! As smoke vanisheth, so let them vanish away: as wax melteth before the fire, so let the wicked perish at the presence of God."

By this time the Easter sun had risen and its morning splendour bathed the beautiful spring garments of the earth. But at the words of Patrick darkness crept once more over the sky and the solid ground shook with a great earthquake. The swords and spears of the warriors clashed upon their shields with dreadful clangour. It seemed to them that the sky was falling down upon the earth, and that there was no hope of escape from impending destruction. The horses took fright and galloped hither and thither in wild confusion, while the wind blew so fiercely that the chariots were whirled away over the plain.

Each warrior rose up against the other in the assembly and they slew one another, so that at least fifty men fell dead upon the field. Then, perceiving their mistake, the survivors fled in all directions, leaving only three persons of all the pagan host. These were King Laeghaire with his Queen Angas, whose royal courage forbade them to seek safety in an ignominious flight; together with one obscure but faithful attendant who would not desert his sovereign in that dire extremity.

When the terror had passed, the king remained sullenly silent, but the queen rose and approached Patrick with words of respect and conciliation on her lips—

"O just and mighty man," she said, "do not destroy the king. For he shall come to thee, and shall do thy will, and shall kneel and believe in God."

Like many a peacemaker, Angas made promises which had but little foundation. So far did her gentle influence prevail, however, and so shaken was the haughty monarch by the events of the last few hours, that he bent the knee before Patrick, offering him peace; though, as we shall see, it was a false peace.

Even before leaving that place Laeghaire made an unsuccessful attempt on Patrick's life, while speaking to him apart. God made the treacherous design known to the Saint, who dexterously evaded the snare. An invitation to Tara was then given with the intention of taking Patrick's life on the way.

"Come after me, O cleric," said the wily king, "that at Tara I may believe in thee in presence of the men of Ireland."

Patrick willingly consented, and straightway Laeghaire gave orders that an ambush should be set on every path from Slane to Tara, so that at one or other Patrick must surely die. The chariots were yoked once more by the attendants who had now returned, and the royal party set out for the palace, weary and crestfallen after their disastrous night in the open.

Patrick and his clerics concluded the interrupted office of Easter Day with due solemnity and with hearts full of gratitude to the risen Lord Who had so wonderfully aided them. It was still early when the Saint chose his companions and blessed them before setting out on their perilous journey. They were eight young clerics and the boy Benignus who never left the side of his dear father, as he called St Patrick. They had ten miles to walk, but "God covered them with a cloak of darkness so that not one of them could be seen. Nevertheless the heathen, as they watched in their hiding places, "beheld eight deer passing by them at the foot of the mountain, and behind the deer was a fawn with a bundle on its shoulder." Patrick was invisible, but the eight deer were his clerics, and Benignus behind them with his tablets strapped to his back.

It was during this memorable journey that St Patrick is supposed to have uttered the pious ejaculations which afterwards took the form so well known as "St Patrick's Breastplate." Its other name, "The Deer's Cry," recalls the picturesque episode of the passage of the eight young clerics round the foot of

Slane Mountain. The Saint in this hymn of praise and petition expresses his firm belief in the Blessed Trinity, the Incarnation, Death, Resurrection, and Ascension of Christ. He unites with the citizens of Heaven, and with all God's creatures in giving glory to Him Who is his defence against the wiles of the devil and against all forms of superstition and idolatry; ending by an appeal to Christ our Lord to be with him always, and to speak to him through every creature.

Meanwhile Laeghaire was sitting in grief and shame in the banqueting hall of Tara, together with the nobles, bards and wizards who had escaped from the slaughter of the previous night. The thought that in his terror he had knelt to Patrick overwhelmed him with humiliation, and he awaited with anxiety the news that his snares had been successful and that the disturber of his peace was no more. Nevertheless, it was a day of high festival, and, however angrily he might brood over his private vexations, he could not refuse the duty of hospitality to invited guests. The great hall was decked out in all its magnificence and the doors being closed the noble company sat down to table, their minds so full of the strange events of the night that no other subject of conversation was broached.

"I will go to Tara," Patrick had said in answer to the king's invitation, "that I may manifest my readiness before the men of Ireland."

Laeghaire had taken measures to secure that, though the Saint should set out on the journey he might never reach its goal. Suddenly, in the midst of the feasting, "Patrick stood there in the hall of Tara, the doors being closed, as when Christ came into the upper room." The Saint had in mind the words of His Divine Master when he said:—

"Neither do men light a candle and put it under a bushel, but upon a candlestick, that it may shine to all that are in the house. So let your light shine before men, that they may see your good works, and glorify your Father Who is in Heaven."

"I will not make of myself a candle under a bushel," said Patrick, "but I must see who it is that will believe in me and who will not believe."

Therefore he stood, serenely confident, in the centre of Tara's hall and waited to see who would first move to greet him.

The happy man who was thus inspired was Dubthach, king-poet of all Ireland, and of King Laeghaire; and his example was followed by a promising stripling of his household named Fiacc. These two rose spontaneously to their feet and did homage to the man of God. Patrick blessed them for their faith, and both became his fervent disciples. But not a man among the other nobles and courtiers present rose up before Patrick, lest they should seem to set at naught the command of the king, or expose themselves to the necessity of embracing the new faith.

Churlish as Laeghaire might be, there was no possibility of setting aside the duty of hospitality which bound the Irish monarch even to an enemy who had obtained access to his banqueting hall. The first moment of surprise having passed, Patrick was summoned to the king's couch that he might partake of food and prove his ability in speech. Knowing the good results that were likely to follow, the Saint accepted the invitation with alacrity. His absolute trust in God rendered him fearless as Daniel in the lions' den, though fierce looks were cast upon him, and deadly enmity was hidden beneath the smooth words of courtesy. Never did his natural gifts shine to greater advantage than in that lordly hall where the High King and his chieftains held their court in royal state. He sat there at his ease, not only in the position of an ambassador of heaven but also as a noble Roman citizen, representative of the great Empire of which all stood in awe, though to it none there present had bent his neck in reverence.

St. Patrick Preaching at Tara.

Lucat-mael, the wizard, whose heart was embittered by Patrick's treatment of his comrade Lochru, hid under a show of hospitable attention a scheme of deadly vengeance. He managed to pour into the cup which stood at Patrick's hand a drop of poison sufficient to destroy a man's life. But the Saint had prayed on his journey that Christ might protect him that day against every poison; and the designs of the wicked wizard were frustrated. Patrick, perceiving the poison, blessed the cup, whereupon the liquor curdled leaving the poison liquid, so that by inverting the cup the drop was easily poured out. Patrick again blessed the cup and the liquor was restored to its proper nature and he drank it in the name of Jesus Christ his Lord. By this miracle God's name and Patrick's were magnified exceedingly.

The banquet over, it was proposed that the company should adjourn to the vast plain below the royal hill. It must have been a great joy to the eight young clerics and the boy Benignus to see their beloved master come forth unhurt from the palace to which, apparently, they had not been admitted. The army of King Laeghaire was drawn up in battle array; the king and queen with their guests and their retinue took their places; all was ready for the trial of strength between Christianity and heathendom, represented on the one hand by Patrick, on the other by Lucat-mael.

"Let us," said the wizard, "work miracles before the host in that great plain."

"What miracles shall we work?" asked Patrick.

"Let us bring snow on the plain, till it is white in front of us," proposed Lucat.

"I have no desire to oppose God's Will," replied Patrick.

"Whether it is thy desire or not," said the wizard, "I will bring snow on the plain."

This he said, having in his power a certain number of

apparent miracles with which to deceive the people. Patrick's seeming indifference probably led the wizard to suppose that snow was not among the Saint's collection of magical effects. Then Lucat-mael began "the chants of wizardry and the rites of devilry," so that snow fell until it reached men's girdles. All the people saw it and marvelled greatly and they applauded the wizard for his wonderful power. This was Patrick's opportunity.

"We see this," he said quietly; "now, put it away if thou canst."

But the wizard was obliged to confess. "I cannot do that, until this hour to-morrow." Patrick was moved to righteous indignation.

"In evil alone does thy power lie," he cried, "and not in good!"

Then leaning upon the Staff of Jesus which he carried in his left hand, and raising his right hand, he blessed the plain in its four quarters, north, south, east and west, in the name of the Father, and of the Son, and of the Holy Ghost. Quicker than speech, at Patrick's word the snow vanished, without rain, or sun, or wind to take it away.

The discomfited wizard had recourse once more to his incantations and brought on a thick darkness which overspread the face of the earth. Those who had been at Slane the night before, remembering their experience, were terrified, and the multitude uttered cries of consternation.

The authoritative voice of Patrick was heard above the tumult.

"Dispel the darkness," he said.

But the wizard gave the same excuse: he must wait for the morrow. Again Patrick prayed and blessed the plain; the darkness rolled away; the sun shone out and all gave thanks to the God of Patrick and to the Saint.

Thus they contended for a long time in the presence of the king and his court, the army and the people. Laeghaire, seeing that his wizard was being vanquished at every point, and impatient for a conclusive trial, proposed that the druidical and the Christian books should be cast into the stream which flowed from the hill of Tara across the plain. The victory was to be given to him whose books should come out of the water undamaged. Patrick was quite willing to accept the test, but the wizard objected.

"Because," he said, "he hath water as a god,"—evidently referring to the Christian custom of baptizing with water.

The king made a new proposal.

"Cast them," he said, "into the fire." Patrick was ready for this trial also. The wizard, however, would not risk his reputation, for, he said—

"This man, turn about in alternate years, venerates as a god now water and now fire," and by fire he meant the gifts of the Holy Ghost.

Patrick denied the accusation of idolatry, but, knowing his power, he did not think it necessary to insist upon his claims.

"That is not so;" he said simply, "but since thou sayest that I adore a god of fire, thou shalt go, if thou art willing, apart into a house completely shut up; and a cleric of my household before thee, and my chasuble around thee; and thy wizard's tunic around my cleric, and fire shall be put to the house, so that God may deal doom on you therein."

The counsel was discussed and approved by the men of Ireland around King Laeghaire. Lucat-mael must have felt that in his present state of humiliation and disgrace it mattered little what befell him. Seeing no escape from the decision he superintended the building of the wooden house, and managed that the part allotted to himself should be of green wood, while that for Patrick's cleric should be dry. But his dishonesty was observed by eyes that could not brook the sight of a mean and treacherous deception.

There were at that time in hostageship to the High King, three youths of royal blood from other kingdoms. They were, of course, as any boys would have been, deeply interested in the spectacle of the curious struggle between Patrick and the wizard. As the workmen built the hut they were all eyes and ears for the work.

Presently they came weeping to Patrick as he sat apart surrounded by his clerics.

"What is the matter, my sons?" asked the Saint with fatherly kindness.

"Alas!" they sighed, "in the chief city of the Gael, a prince's troth hath this day been broken."

"How has this happened?" inquired Patrick, with a smile of encouragement.

"The house which is being built," said the princes, "for the wizard and thy servant, is one half of fresh wood and the other of dry and withered wood; the fresh being for the wizard, and the dry for thy servant."

So saying they continued to weep at this dastardly abuse of the royal power. But Patrick, undisturbed, put his finger on the right cheek of each child and took from it a tear which he placed in his left palm. Then he breathed upon the tears, and they became three lovely gems. The boys were greatly comforted, for they saw plainly that Patrick had no fears for the result of his trial in spite of the wizard's treachery.

"Swallow the gems," said Patrick. They willingly did as they were told.

Then the Saint, turning to his disciples spoke this prophecy.

"Three noble and venerable gems shall come of these children, namely, Columbcille, and Comgall of Bangor, and Finden of Movilla."

Meanwhile the house was built and all was ready. Among his clerics Patrick chose the sweet boy Benignus who would have gone to death for the love of God and his dear master, but who was too full of trust to think that harm could come to him when the Saint was nigh. He was clothed in the wizard's tunic and took his place in the dry part of the hut. "Then the wizard entered the other side with Patrick's chasuble round him, and the door was closed upon the two, a bar being set upon it outside for all the host to see." Fire was applied to the wood, but, contrary to all expectation and by an evident miracle, the fresh part of the house, with the wizard in it was burnt to ashes, Patrick's chasuble alone remaining intact. No efforts could avail to set the dry part on fire, but the wizard's tunic caught the flame and was consumed, though Benignus, who wore it, was unscathed.

Great was the anger of King Laeghaire when he saw himself thus deprived of his second wizard. He started to his feet and would have slain Patrick instantly with his own hand, had he not been prevented by the power of God.

"Unless thou believest now," said Patrick, "thou shalt die quickly, for God's anger will come upon thy head."

The king was seized with over-mastering fear at these words, and he went into his council-chamber and said to those around him—

"In my opinion belief in God is better than what is threatened to me, namely, that I shall die presently."

So once more Laeghaire knelt to Patrick and professed belief for fear of death. Many thousands were that day baptized as a consequence of the king's example, and the faith grew and prospered, for Laeghaire gave liberal permission for preaching it throughout the land, promising protection to the missionaries as long as he lived and reigned.

"In this legend of Patrick's dealings with the High King, "says Professor Bury, "there is one implication which harmonises with other records, and which, we cannot doubt, reflects, while it distorts, a fact. Patrick visited Laeghaire in his palace at Tara, but he went as a guest in peace, not as a hostile magician and a destroyer of life. The position which the Christian creed had won rendered a conference no less desirable for the High King than for the Bishop who represented the Church of the Empire. Laeghaire agreed to protect Patrick in his own kingdom though he resisted any attempts that were made to convert him."

Patrick and Laeghaire are, then, the real personages in the drama. The two druids are but personifications of different kinds of resistance made by paganism: Lochru, violent, clamorous and blasphemous, dashed to pieces against the rock of Truth; Lucat-mael, the type of subtle cunning and the secret poison of calumny, consumed and annihilated in those flames of which Christ says, "I have come to cast fire upon the earth, and what will I but that it be kindled?"

"So the meek believed, and the wise, and brave,
 And Mary's Son as their God adored.
And the druids, because they could answer nought,
Bowed down to the Faith the stranger brought.
That day on Erin God poured His Spirit:
Yet none like the chief of the bards had merit,
Dubthach! He rose and believed the first
Ere the great light yet on the rest had burst."
 It was thus that Erin, then blind but strong,
 To Christ through her chief bard paid homage due:
 And this was a sign that in Erin song
 Should from first to last to the Cross be true."

Chapter VI

From East to West

A FEW miles from Tara, at the spot where the town of Trim now stands, a son of King Laeghaire had his fort or dun. Prince Fedilmid, for so he was called, was a man of noble and generous character, and his many good qualities made him a fit husband for the fair young British princess who had left her country to become his wife. Fedilmid's mother had also been a British lady whose name has been recorded in history as Scoth Noe, or the Fresh Flower.

Some account of this noble couple may have reached the priest Lomman, Patrick's nephew, who had been left in charge of the boat at the mouth of the Boyne. According to directions, Lomman and his companions sailed up the river, and reaching Trim at nightfall, they moored their boat and rested there till dawn. The place was called the Ford of the Alder tree and was so lovely that in the morning the missionaries lingered there to say Mass and to recite the canonical hours.

It was an Irish custom in those primitive times to bathe in warm water, using soap and linen towels, at night before retiring to rest, and in the morning merely to wash the face and hands, "for which purpose," says Joyce, "they generally went out immediately after rising and dressing, to some well or stream near the house." This will explain how it was that Fedilmid's young son, Fortchern, in the British tongue, Vortigern, came running down to the river at an early hour. Great was the boy's surprise when he saw the boat, the clerics, and Lomman, who, with the book of the gospels open before him was telling of Christ and the good tidings of salvation for all.

The prince listened and marvelled, this doctrine appealed to his naturally Christian soul and satisfied his heart. He believed; and, approaching Lomman, begged to be admitted into the company of those who served Christ. The favour was readily granted; the waters of baptism cleansed that privileged soul from original sin, and Fortchern became one of the most fervent and enthusiastic followers of the missionaries.

The princess, going later in search of her son, found him in the holy assembly listening with rapt attention to Lomman's words, his bright face glowing with the radiance of his recent baptism. The accents of the British priest fell sweetly on her ear so long accustomed to a foreign tongue. With great cordiality she welcomed the party to her husband's fort and then hurried home to tell Fedilmid the news and prepare for the arrival of their guests.

The prince was equally pleased to hear of British strangers, countrymen of his mother and his wife. He went to meet them and he also believed, so that the entire household was gained to Christ. Fortchern was allowed by his parents to follow the vocation to the priesthood with which God had favoured him and, in his generous fervour, Fedilmid gave Trim for ever to God, to Patrick, to Lomman and to Fortchern. But so detached was Fortchern from earthly things that afterwards, when appointed second bishop of Trim on the death of Lomman, he resigned the See, lest he should seem to favour the succession of bishops to hereditary domains.

We may suppose that Lomman and the new Christians

were anxious to have Patrick among them, and that Fedilmid sent chariots to convey the Saint to Trim on the evening of the wonderful Easter Sunday which had seen the defeat of wizardry in its head-quarters. Patrick seems to have had no intention of returning to Slane, and Trim was nearer; moreover, there he would find friendly hospitality and some repose after his labours. Certain it is that he came in person to found the church of Trim and to consecrate Lomman as its first Bishop. This church in later times became one of the most celebrated sanctuaries of Our Lady in Ireland, the shrine of a miraculous statue honoured throughout the land, and a place of perpetual pilgrimage.

The gathering of notables at Tara which Patrick had found so opportune for the preaching of the Gospel, was followed by national festivities at the place now known as Telltown. The Saint resolved to be present at the meeting, there to urge his claims on the faith of the people. The journey was not a long one, but it was beset with peril, for this part of the country belonged to a son of Niall, named Cairbre, who was as much opposed to Christianity as was his brother Laeghaire. The wicked prince sought Patrick that he might put him to death. He intercepted some of the Saint's followers for the purpose of finding out the direction in which he had gone. On their refusal to betray their master, he had them cruelly scourged but without being able to obtain the information he asked for. Patrick escaped all the snares laid for him, and was wont to speak of Cairbre as God's foe and as a man who would be chastised for his crimes.

A very different reception awaited the Apostle on the part of Conall, another son of Niall, who joyfully heard the Word of God and embraced the faith. Patrick blessed him and promised him prosperity and dominion over his wicked brother, Cairbre. Conall bestowed on Patrick a portion of land on which to build a church, thenceforth known as Donagh Patrick.

The visit to Telltown was partly frustrated by the machinations of Cairbre, but Patrick blessed the plain on which the assembly was held, preaching, meanwhile, to all who would listen to his words. He passed the rest of this year, 433, in ceaseless journeyings in Meath, founding churches where he was well received and threatening God's vengeance on refractory chieftains with such effect that they dared not prevent their people from becoming Christians.

A merciless man once resisted all Patrick's endeavours and continued to practise cruelty and oppression. The Saint took the Staff of Jesus and with it marked out a cross on a flagstone. The stone was cut as if it had been soft clay.

"If I were not patient with thee," said Patrick, "the might of God's power would cleave thee as the crozier cleft the stone."

Those proud chieftains who would not embrace the faith for the love of God, often yielded to fear, and the prince once subdued, it was easy to win the people. As he proceeded westward from Meath, the Saint pursued his usual policy of setting up his tents near the local fortress by the side of some spring or stream of water to be used as a baptismal font. He was generally warmly welcomed and obtained a piece of ground on which to build a church; if he was driven away, as happened sometimes, he sought a more hospitable locality.

Journeying thus in easy stages he came to a place called Mag Slecht, renowned as a strong hold of idolatry and demonolatry. Hither King Laeghaire had himself come, in spite of his recent profession of Christianity, in order to propitiate the demon god who dwelt in Crom-Cruach. This was the chief idol of Ireland, an enormous stone, standing upright covered with plates of gold and silver offered by the benighted pagans. Round about Crom-Cruach stood twelve smaller stones encased in brass, and there great crowds of people high and low would come and prostrate themselves in abject worship.

From the elevated ground on which the idols stood there gushed a stream of water flowing between green banks on its winding way through the plain. Patrick was following the course of this stream, when suddenly at a turning he came within view of—

> "The nation's idol, lifting high
> His head, and those twelve vassal-gods around
> All mailed in gold, and shining as the sun,
> A pomp impure."

Shocked at the sight of the grovelling multitude, Patrick raised his powerful voice in an indignant cry that was heard all over the plain a cry so heart-piercing that the place was afterwards called Guthard or "The Great Shout." All eyes were turned towards the procession of clerics in which the impressive figure of Patrick was easily distinguishable. In his hand he carried the Staff of Jesus, and raising it he struck a blow at Crom-Cruach. Though the Saint was too far away to touch the idol, it fell instantly on its right side, while on its left, visible to all who chose to look, was the indentation made by the crozier, though it had not moved from Patrick's hand.

Then the earth was convulsed, and swallowed up the twelve smaller idols, leaving only their heads above the ground as a memorial of their fate. But Crom-Cruach lay there until Patrick came and exorcised the demon which had long inhabited it. Nor did the evil spirit leave the huge stone without a frightful exhibition of his power. The form in which he appeared was so hideous that all present thought their last hour had surely come and that they must fall victims to his malignant influence. Not so Patrick. Serene and undaunted, he cursed the demon, and commanded him to return forthwith to hell, and no more to trouble the people. His words banished the evil spirit, and the terrible scene was followed by peace and calm, both in the elements and in the minds of those present.

Laeghaire saw the ignominious end of his great idol with feelings of terror and remorse, but with out any intention of abjuring paganism. He was a man of a fixed idea, and nothing could change him. His own words explain the obstinacy which would otherwise be incomprehensible.

"Niall," said he, "my father, when he heard the false prophecy of the coming of the Faith, enjoined us not to believe, but he said that I should be buried in the topmost part of Tara, like warlike men." It was the custom of the heathen kings to be buried in an erect position, armed, and with their faces turned in the direction of their enemies, to express their undying hatred. Now, Niall knew that Christianity would give no countenance to such uncharitableness, and it was for this that he laid upon his successor the command that was to cost him so dear.

Crom-Cruach was vanquished, but Patrick found that by his strenuous exertions, he had loosened the brooch which held his mantle. There is a homely touch about his anxious search for the missing article at such a moment of triumph. His followers came to his aid, but it was not until they had cleared the place of the herbage growing upon it, that they recovered the brooch, which would have been no small loss, if it was of the elaborate kind described by Irish antiquarians.

Patrick founded a church in that place, called Domnach Mag Slecht, and he appointed as its pastor a relative of his own, Mabran, surnamed Barbarus, whom they used to call "Patrick's Barbarian," not because he was uncivilised, but on account of his not being, like most of the clerics, a Roman citizen. The waters flowing from the idol hill were thereafter called "Patrick's Well," because in them the Saint had baptized the multitudes converted by that day's miraculous events.

Faring ever westward the Apostle crossed the Shannon, and found himself in Connaught, which, like Meath, was ruled by brothers and sons of Niall the Great. Suddenly the noonday sun was obscured and the missionaries were enveloped in a preternatural darkness. Patrick knew well that it came from the machinations of the druids of those parts. Having advanced but slowly for three days, the Saint made up his mind to put an end to the plague. He knelt down, therefore, and begged of God to hear his prayer, and to deliver His servants from "every cruel and merciless power; the incantations of false prophets, black laws of the heathen, craft of idolatry and spells of wizards." Then, making the sign of the cross over the plain, he caused daylight to shine once more, the wizards alone remaining in darkness. And Patrick gave thanks to God that the darkness was banished at his prayer.

The prime authors of this darkness were two brother wizards, Mael and Caplait, who had heard of the progress Patrick was making, and who had invoked the aid of their demons in order to frustrate his plans. King Laeghaire had confided to these two learned men the education of his youngest daughters, Fedelm the Rosy and Ethne the Fair. They were intelligent and beautiful maidens, worthy of their royal race, gentle and sportive as young gazelles. According to the custom we have already seen observed by Prince Fortchern, they ran down each morning to the waterside to wash their hands and faces in the running stream.

It happened one morning that the missionaries being in the neighbourhood, assembled round the well, Clebach, at sunrise to celebrate the divine office. Clad in their white robes, and holding their holy books from which they read or sang, they looked like a company of noble princes, with Patrick their master at their head, holding in his hand his crozier, the Staff of Jesus.

The two princesses were suddenly brought to a standstill

when, on their way to the well, they beheld this unlooked-for sight. The druids, their tutors, had carefully concealed from them all knowledge of the Christian religion; the maidens, therefore, were greatly perplexed at this vision of persons such as they had never seen or even heard of. In a country whose very atmosphere breathed poetry and legendary lore it was not unnatural that the idea of fairy-men, or gods of the earth, or even ghosts should spring to their minds, and set their young imaginations on fire.

As for fear, it was a sentiment unknown to these daughters of the High King of Ireland.

"Whence are ye and whence have ye come?" cried Fedelm.

"Are ye of the elves or of the gods?" asked Ethne.

Then Patrick, gently and gravely, smiling a little, perhaps, at their artless eagerness, went straight to the point, sweeping aside all superstitious thoughts:—

"It were better for you," he said, "to believe in God than to inquire about our race."

This was mysterious language to maidens who had been brought up in utter ignorance of the one true God. The elder of the two plied the stranger with questions.

"Who is your God, and where is He?" she asked. "Is He in Heaven, or in earth, or under earth, or on earth? Is He in seas, or in streams, or in mountains, or in glens? Hath He sons and daughters? Is there gold and silver, is there abundance of every good thing in His Kingdom? O tell us about Him," she continued, growing more and more inflamed with the desire of knowing Him Whose grace was working in her soul—"tell us how He is seen, how He is loved, how He is found—if He is in youth or if He is in age—if He is everliving, if He is beautiful—if many have fostered His sons, if His daughters are dear and beautiful to the people of the world."

There was something of inspiration in the language of the

lovely young pagan. Patrick heard her patiently until, out of breath, she paused and waited for his reply. Filled with the joy of the Holy Spirit at the glorious opportunity afforded him, he gave the maidens a simple and clear instruction in the elements of the Christian Faith. They seated themselves to listen in rapt astonishment.

"Our God is the God of all things," he began, "the God of heaven, and earth, and sea and river; the God of sun and moon and all the stars; the God of high mountains and lowly valleys; the God over heaven, and in heaven, and under heaven. He hath a dwelling both in heaven and earth and sea, and all that is therein. He inspires all things. He gives life to all things; He surpasses all things, He sustains all things. He kindles the light of the sun and the light of the moon. He made springs in arid land, and dry islands in the sea; and stars He appointed to minister to the greater lights."

Having thus impressed the minds of his hearers with the hitherto unsuspected notion of one only true and living God, the Apostle went on to show that there was a yet deeper mystery to be believed rather than understood. This omnipotent and eternal God is One, yet He is Three.

"He hath a Son," continued Patrick, "co-eternal with Himself, and like unto Him. But the Son is not younger than the Father, nor the Father older than the Son. And the Holy Spirit breathes in Them. Father and Son and Holy Spirit are not divided."

Did Patrick illustrate his teaching on this occasion by plucking a leaf of shamrock and pointing to its threefold unity? We do not know, for the chroniclers are silent as to the particular moment of this happy inspiration. It is, however, likely that he often brought home to his simple audience the truths of faith by familiar objects. In the case of these royal maidens there was little need of insistence—they had given their confidence to the Herald of the King, and he had but to speak to obtain their absolute and unswerving belief. He understood their aspirations, and he raised their thoughts higher still.

"Howbeit," he said, "I desire to unite you to the Son of the heavenly King, for ye are daughters of a king of earth. "

No need was there to enlarge upon the wonderful deeds of the Son of heaven's King. His Incarnation, Life, Death and Resurrection, were all contained in the implicit act of faith in which their hearts leaped out towards the Triune God. They exclaimed, as it were, with one mouth and one heart:—

"How shall we be able to believe in that King? Teach us most diligently that we may see the Lord face to face. Teach us the way and we will do whatsoever thou shalt say unto us."

Sin being the chief obstacle to their desire to be united to God, Patrick proceeded to instruct them in the doctrine of its forgiveness by the Sacraments of Baptism and Penance. Then he said:—

"Do you believe that through Baptism the sin of your first parents is put away from you?"

"We believe," they answered fervently.

"Do you believe in the remedy of repentance after sin? "

"We believe."

Having thus made their profession of faith, they were baptized; and Patrick blessed the white veil of their virginity, placing it upon each fair young head as the symbol of their espousals to the Son of the Great King. Nothing would now satisfy them but the beatific vision itself. They repeated their request that they might be allowed to see Christ face to face. This was the fitting moment for making known to them the mystery of the Holy Eucharist.

"Ye cannot see Christ," said Patrick, "unless ye first taste of death, and unless ye receive Christ's Body and Blood."

And the maidens answered:—

"Give us the Eucharist that we may be able to see the Spouse."

> " 'Give us the Sacrifice!' Each bright head
> Bent towards it as sunflowers bend to the sun:
> They ate; and the blood from the warm cheeks fled;
> The exile was over: the home was won.
> In death they smiled as though on the breast
> Of the Mother Maid they had found their rest."

Thus they fell asleep in death, going in their fresh baptismal innocence and holy dispositions, straight to the everlasting bliss of heaven. Then arose great wailing and lamentation. Their tutors, the druids, were exceedingly angry, and they contended against Patrick, reproaching him for having revealed the Faith to the maidens, and for being the cause of their untimely death.

Caplait, in particular, who had been the guardian of the younger girl, came crying against Patrick, and bitterly upbraided him. Full of sympathy for the heart-stricken grief of the man who had so lovingly tended that sweet child, Patrick spoke soothingly to him, and gently remonstrated with him for grudging her the happiness she now enjoyed in the kingdom of Christ. Caplait had a mind capable of grasping the truths of Christianity. He asked for baptism, and, seeing his good dispositions, Patrick tonsured him and took him into the number of his disciples.

Thereupon Mael was moved to indignation. He came to Patrick, saying:—

"My brother hath believed in thee, but no advantage shalt thou have out of him. I will bring him back into heathenism."

Thus wrathfully he spoke before the people, endeavouring to disgrace Patrick in their sight. Soon, however, the meekness of the Saint, and the sweetness and power of the gospel teaching won his heart also; and he believed and was baptized, and Patrick tonsured him, so that there came to be a proverb, "Mael is like unto Caplait," referring to the unity of their belief, and to the tonsure worn by both.

The days of the lamentation for the death of the princesses being at an end, they were buried in that place, and a church was built there; but some say that the relics of the two young virgins were afterwards taken to Armagh, and that there they await the resurrection. We are not told what King Laeghaire did or said when he heard that baptism had opened heaven to his daughters. He dared not take any measures against the Saint lest further misfortunes should come upon him; besides this, he had made a solemn promise that no harm should come to Patrick during his reign, and he could not break his royal word.

It makes but little difference to the force of this story if, as Professor Bury contends, there was but one druid, who, from the tonsure of his office, as it existed in Ireland, was called Mael, or the Bald. If it was so, he became, on receiving the tonsure of a Christian cleric, "Capillatus," in Irish Caplait. One, or both, received the grace of conversion, and the proverb fitted the case or perhaps produced the story. That the incident is founded on fact seems clear to Bury, who says, "We can hardly escape the inference that the maidens were in truth daughters of Laeghaire. Such an identification was not at all likely to have been invented by popular legend. In sending children to be brought up away from their home, King Laeghaire would have followed the general practice of the country, and that he should have sent them to the royal residence of Connaught, would have been natural enough. The fathers of King Amalgaid and King Laeghaire were brothers."

The record of Patrick's journeyings up and down through Connaught during these years is but a list of difficult names, broken here and there by a slight incident. It is even said that what is spoken of by the chroniclers as one visit was in reality

St. Patrick showing the People the Book of the Four Gospels.

three, so that there is no certainty as to the sequence of events. The same may be said of much that we relate, but as there is no possibility of restoring the narrative to its true perspective, at this distance of time, we must leave it as it is and be thankful that so much has been handed down to us.

Patrick founded a church at Cell Garad, now called Oran, and there he had a well dug for the purpose of baptizing the people. He loved the waters of this well very dearly, and, weary as he often was with his continual wanderings in search of souls, he would gladly have taken up his abode, at least for a time, in that quiet spot. He sang in its praise a sorrowful little song which has been translated thus:—

> "Uaran Gar!
> Uaran which I have loved; which loved me!
> Sad is my cry, O dear God,
> Without my drink out of Uaran Gar!
> Cold Uaran!
> Cold (with sorrow) is everyone who has gone from it:
> Were it not my King's command,
> I would not wend from it, though the weather is cold.
> Thrice I went into the land:
> Three fifties, this was my number,
> For with thee
> Was my consolation, Uaran!"

Thrice, as he says, in the land of Connaught, he passed up and down over the stony soil, accompanied by his three fifties, or one hundred and fifty disciples, many of them youths, like Benignus, and Mochae, and Fortchern, in course of training for the priesthood; others, like those called "Patrick's Franks," clerics who had come from Gaul or Britain to aid him. There was little time or opportunity for lingering by the cool waters of Uaran Gar, when so great a harvest of souls awaited the outpouring of God's grace. In spite of weariness, he pressed on to the work that ever increased before him.

At Drumana Patrick had the happiness of giving the

religious veil to a holy virgin, known in the Irish calendar as St Attracta. She was the daughter of a nobleman named Talan, who seems to have given land for a church, with a convent for nuns attached to it, of which St Attracta was the first abbess. Patrick provided a paten and a chalice, with other necessaries for the Holy Sacrifice. When the Saint had blessed the veil to be placed on Attracta's head, a chasuble came down from heaven and rested on Patrick's bosom.

"Let the chasuble be thine, O nun," said Patrick, thinking of the new church.

"Not so," said she, "not unto me hath it been given, but unto thy goodness."

It is not recorded to which of the two Saints the miraculous chasuble remained, but the argument of St Attracta was certainly the stronger. She governed her abbey with piety and wisdom, with glory to God and edification to men, until her holy death. The fame of her sanctity was perpetuated in the churches and miraculous wells to which her name was given. The number of Irish maidens who dedicated themselves to God at the preaching of Patrick, will only be known in heaven, but a few names, like those of Fedelm, and Ethne, and Attracta, have been registered in the pages of history.

One day, as Patrick reached the brow of a hill, he caught sight of two men fighting desperately with swords. Full of concern he inquired into the cause of their quarrel, and was told that they were brothers, whose father in dying had left a piece of land, which was the origin of their dispute. The Saint raised his hand and made the sign of the cross over the combatants. Immediately the right arm of each grew stiff, and though his hand still grasped his sword, he was unable to stretch it out or to draw it in.

"Sit down," said Patrick. All seated themselves, and the Saint heard the complaints of the two brothers, made peace between them, and gave them his blessing. Thereupon they were filled with gratitude, and they asked Patrick to take the ground and build a church upon it for the sake of their father's soul. This he did, and appointed Conu the Wright, brother of Sechnall, to be its pastor.

When Patrick had preached to the men of Umall and converted them, he consecrated Senach to rule over them. The meekness and innocence of this holy man reminded Patrick so much of Our Lord's title of the Lamb of God, that he was wont to call him affectionately "Agnus Dei." Before his consecration, Senach asked three boons of Patrick: the first, that from that time forward he might not in any way offend God; the second, that his diocese should not be called by his name; the third, that the years which might be wanting to him at his death should be given to his son Oengus. For Senach had been married and had two children, Oengus and Mathona, the former of whom was trained by Patrick for the priesthood, and the latter invested with the cloak and veil of a consecrated virgin.

This church of Senach at Aghagower was, like Uaran Gar, the scene of one of Patrick's temptations to weariness and lassitude. He longed to be at rest, free from the awful responsibilities of his mission, and able to give himself up to his favourite occupation of contemplating God in solitude. Again he sang a little song:—

> "I would choose
> To remain here on a little land,
> After faring around churches and waters,
> Since I am weary I would not go further."

The founding of churches and the innumerable baptisms, however consoling, was to nature most fatiguing; grace had to come to the assistance of the worn-out Apostle. Like the angel who came to comfort Our Lord in His agony, Victor came to Patrick and buoyed up his fainting courage with bright promises of reward:—

> "Thou shalt have everything round which thou shalt go,
>> Every land,
>> Both mountains and churches,
>> Both glens and woods,
> After faring around churches and waters,
> Though thou art weary, still shalt thou go on further."

Thus encouraged, the blessed Apostle prepared to set out once more on the journeys which were to make the whole island his own for God's great glory and the salvation of untold thousands of souls. Climbing mountains, crossing bogs, fording rivers, sleeping in the open, beaten by wind and hail, drenched by rain and snow, a victim to all the caprices of the elements, not to speak of the opposition and the snares of wicked men, Patrick had before him a task requiring indomitable courage. At his departure from Aghagower he left there as a memorial of his love for its waters, two small trout in the well, blessing them and promising that angels would keep them in it for ever. Leaving that quiet spot,

> "Not once he turned,
> Climbing the uplands rough, or crossing streams
> Swoll'n by the melting snows. The Brethren paced
> Behind; Benignus first, his psalmist; next
> Sechnall, his bishop; next his brehon, Erc;
> Mochta, his priest; and Sinell of the bells;
> Rodan, his shepherd; Essa, Bite, and Tassach,
> Workers of might in iron and in stone,
> God-taught, to build the churches of the faith
> With wisdom and with heart-delighting craft;
> MacCartan last, the giant meek that oft
> On shoulders broad bore Patrick through the floods."

Chapter VII

Patrick's Prayers and Devotions

T PATRICK was the Apostle of what was to be an apostolic nation—a nation which should scatter its children abroad over the face of the earth for the extension of Catholic Christianity throughout the ages. This is an undeniable fact; and, looking back, we cannot fail to see how necessary it was for its accomplishment that the faith should be securely planted, and that there should be no doubt of Ireland's unswerving fidelity to the teachings of her great master in Christ.

It was in all humility, with deep distrust of himself and firm confidence in God, that Patrick applied himself to his task. "I commend my soul," he writes in his "Confession," "to my most faithful God, Whose ambassador I am in my lowliness, only because He accepteth no person and He chose me for this office that I should be His minister, but amongst the least."

Such was Patrick's own judgment of himself and his mission; not so, however, that of his biographers. It may be that they allowed themselves to be carried away by enthusiasm and by their admiration for Patrick's wonderful gift of prayer, and the favours by which it was rewarded. But, apart from all flights of imagination, there remains the permanent miracle to which every priest can testify, that souls, for whom all hope seemed lost, return to God and take their flight to heaven from even the most forsaken Irish deathbeds.

We cannot doubt that St Patrick prayed most efficaciously for the spiritual perseverance of his flock. In his zeal for the salvation of the men of Ireland, he wrestled, not merely with the powers of darkness, but, like Jacob, with an angel of light, if we are to believe the legend of Mount Cruachan. He held St Victor, and he would not let him go until he blessed him and obtained for him all the gifts he asked for the people of his choice. This much we may accept as certain, and it is the basis on which the legend rests. But we know that St Patrick was alone with God, the angels, and the demons, and we may be quite sure that he was incapable of giving the details which have come down to us from the old writers.

His real sentiments are admirably expressed in his own words:—"I ought greatly with fear and trembling to dread that sentence on the day when no one shall be able to absent or conceal himself, but when all of us, every one, shall have to give an account of even his smallest sins before the judgment seat of Christ Our Lord."

Patrick's prayers were powerful because his humility was great. His chroniclers, seeing the effect, failed to penetrate to its cause. Hence their high admiration for what they perceived, and their attempts to account for it in stories like their version of his forty days' fast on Croagh Patrick. We shall, nevertheless, give the legend, partly in their words, and partly in the inspiring verse of Aubrey de Vere.

"Who shall understand the greatness of his diligence in prayer?" exclaims one writer. "For whether he was staying in one place or going on a journey, he used to chant every day psalms and hymns and the spiritual canticles of the Scriptures."

As a youthful slave, while his soul was passing through the trials of the purgative life, he learnt some of the secrets of heavenly contemplation; as a monk, he trod the illuminative paths where God is at all times very near; as a missionary, withdrawing whenever it was possible into the innermost recesses of the unitive sanctuary, he lost himself therein; then, coming forth from behind the veil, he walked in the midst of crowds, like Abraham, with God, as a beloved son with his most dear Father.

The simple confidence he felt in God's infinite goodness and power sometimes seemed to those about him almost like the temerity and importunity of a spoilt child, and it was thus that they represented it. In a manner they were right. Certain that what he asked was according to the Heart of Christ, he continued his supplications and penances until all his requests were granted. Their ignorance of his real methods led his chroniclers to give a symbolical representation of the perseverance and efficacy of his prayers; in any case the prayers were made, and what the Saint asked for was granted.

Nothing was too good for the souls Patrick had come to save. Therefore he fasted, and wept, and laid siege to heaven, hoping that by this holy violence he might open its gates still more widely to the people he loved. His demands were great, but he was labouring for Christ, and like Christ, who "in the days of His flesh with a strong cry and tears, offering up prayers and supplications, was heard for His reverence," Patrick strove with the divine justice, "and became to all who obey him the cause of eternal salvation." Hence we find him on the mountain top, watching and fasting like another Moses; wrestling with an angel like Jacob; but, above all, offering and sacrificing his entire being like Our Lord Himself, for the rescue of immortal souls from the power of Satan.

The cone-shaped mountain now called Croagh Patrick, rising in solitary beauty beside the "Western Sea," was chosen by the Saint for his retreat during one of the Lenten seasons he passed in Connaught.

> "Huge Cruachan, that o'er the western deep
> Hung through sea-mist, with shadowing crag on crag,
> High ridged, and dateless forest, long since dead.
> That forest reached, the angel of the Lord
> Beside him, as he entered, stood and spake:
> 'The gifts thy soul demands, demand them not;
> For they are mighty and immeasurable,
> And over great for granting.' And the Saint:
> 'This mountain Cruachan I will not leave
> Alive till all be granted, to the last.' "

Here, therefore, he abode in great anxiety of soul, without food or drink, from "Shrove Saturday" to Holy Saturday. The mountain peak afforded him a view, unequalled in extent and impressiveness of the land he had come to evangelize; and of the mighty Atlantic, over whose waves so many thousands of his children were to carry the faith, in years to come, towards the vast continent whose existence was still undreamt of in Europe.

> "Far below
> Basking the island lay, through rainbow shower
> Gleaming in part, with shadowy moor, and ridge
> Blue in the distance looming. Westward stretched
> A galaxy of isles, and, these beyond
> Infinite sea, with sacred light ablaze."

In solitude, fasting and prayer, the days wore on; and, as Lent was drawing to a close, the demons resolved to make a final terrific effort to conquer that will which was bent upon driving them from their stronghold. Taking the form of hideous black birds, they covered the mountain and filled the air, so that neither earth nor sky was visible. Patrick took refuge in his usual defence, the words of Holy Scripture. This time, however,

St. Patrick's Temptation.

it was in vain that he chanted maledictive psalms; the demons heeded them not. It was only when he seized his holy bell and rang it loudly, flinging it among them in the end, that they took to flight and came no more to Erin. But they had succeeded in bringing the Saint to the verge of despair, and—

> "He, their conqueror, wept, upon that height
> Standing; nor of his victory had he joy.
> . . . and weeping, still he wept
> Till drenched was all his sad monastic cowl."

In this extremity he was supported and comforted by his angel, who, appearing in human form, dried his tears, and—

> "Putting forth his hand, with living coal
> Snatched from God's altar, made that dripping cowl
> Dry as an autumn sheaf."

Beautiful white birds came flocking round him, singing sweet melodies, and consoling him with the thought that they represented the souls of Irish saints throughout all time. For his further comfort, the angel promised Patrick that he should save from the torments of hell the souls of as many men as would fill the space across the sea as far as his eye could reach.

This was much, but it did not satisfy the Saint's desires. The divine consolations had restored his sinking spirits, and he was ready to fight again courageously for all that could be obtained from God.

> "And Patrick made reply: Not great thy boon!
> Watch have I kept, and wearied are mine eyes,
> And dim; nor see they far o'er yonder deep.' "

"Then thou shalt have both sea and land," replied the angel.

"Is there aught else that God granteth me besides that?" he asked.

"There is," replied the angel. "Seven persons on every Saturday till doom shall be saved from hell's pains through thee."

The Saint was determined to secure special safeguards for those who had been his constant and faithful companions in his missionary labours.

"If God should give aught to me," he said, "let my twelve men be given."

"Thou shalt have them," said the angel, "and now get thee gone from the Rick."

But Patrick was not to be so easily dismissed after all he had suffered.

"I will not get me gone," he declared, "since I have been so grievously tormented, until I receive yet greater favours. Is there anything else that will be given to me?"

"There is," replied the angel. "Thou shalt have safe from hell's pains seven souls every Thursday and twelve every Saturday. And now get thee gone from the Rick."

These concessions had been obtained with so little trouble that Patrick was encouraged to ask for more. He would, at any rate, lose nothing by a refusal.

"I will not get me gone," he reiterated, "since I have been tormented, until I am blessed. Is there anything else that may be granted to me?"

"There is," said the angel, "a great sea-wave shall come over Ireland seven years before the Judgment; and now, get thee gone from the Rick."

The gifts granted to Patrick so far had been gratuitous favours; he had not been asked whether he wanted any particular boon of his own choosing. Hence, he declined to move until he had reached the extreme limit of his privileges.

"I will not get me gone," he said, "since I have been tormented, until I am blessed."

"Is there aught else that thou wouldst demand?" asked the angel.

"There is," said Patrick, "that the Saxons should not dwell

in Ireland by consent or by force, so long as I abide in heaven."

"Thou shalt have this," said the angel.

Lest there should be any misunderstanding, we may explain that, by the Saxons Patrick meant the pagan marauders who were then the terror of the western islands, and who afterwards conquered Britain and uprooted the ancient British Christianity. They never entered Ireland.

Still Patrick refused to go down from the Rick.

"Is there aught else God granteth to me?" he inquired.

"There is," said the angel. "Everyone who shall sing thy hymn (composed by Sechnall) from one watch to the other, that is, between sunset and sunset, shall not have pain or torture."

But the Saint, ever practical, knew that, for many who could not read, it would be impossible to comply with this condition.

"The hymn is long and difficult to remember," he objected.

"Well, then," said the angel, "whosoever shall sing it from 'Christus illum' to the end, and everyone who shall give anything in thy name, and everyone who shall do penance in Ireland, his soul shall not go to hell. And now get thee gone from the Rick."

"I will not get me gone, since I have been tormented, until I am blessed," said Patrick. "Is there aught else?"

"There is," said the angel; "a man for every hair of thy chasuble thou shalt bring out of pains on the day of doom."

But Patrick was not satisfied, although his habit must have represented a large number of souls. He was moved to a holy jealousy of other apostles, and was determined that his people should have greater privileges than any other.

"Which of the other saints who labour for God will not bring that number into heaven?" he asked almost derisively. "Verily I will not take that."

"What wilt thou take?" said the angel meekly.

"That is not hard to say," replied Patrick. "Not one, but

seven, persons for every hair in my chasuble must be saved from hell on the day of Judgment."

"Thou shall have this," said the angel, "and now get thee gone from the Rick."

"I will not get me gone," repeated the Saint.

"Then thou shalt be taken away by force," threatened Victor.

"Since I have been tormented," said Patrick once more, "I will not get me gone until I am blessed, save only if the High King of the seven heavens Himself should come and bid me go."

"Is there something else that thou wouldst demand?" inquired the angel.

"There is," replied Patrick, bracing himself for the most daring request of all. "On the day that the twelve thrones shall be on the mount, when the four rivers of fire shall be around it, and the three households shall be there, namely, the household of heaven, the household of earth, and the household of hell, let me myself be judge over the men of Ireland on that day."

This was so unheard-of a request that the angel could only answer:

"Assuredly, that is a favour not to be obtained from the Lord."

"Unless it be obtained from Him," said Patrick decidedly, "departure from this Rick shall not be obtained from me, from to-day till doom; and, what is more, I shall leave a guardian here."

> "Then heavenward sped
> Victor, God's angel, and the Man of God
> Turned to his offering; and all day he stood
> Offering in heart that offering undefiled
> Which Abel offered and Melchisedech."

Patrick continued in prayer until evening when—

> "By his side
> That angel stood. Then Patrick turning not
> His eyes in prayer upon the West close held

The Angel Victor appearing to St. Patrick.

Demanded, 'From the Maker of all worlds
What answer bring'st thou? Victor made reply:
'Down knelt in Heaven the angelic orders nine,
And all the prophets and the apostles knelt
And all the creatures of the hand of God,
Visible and invisible, down knelt
While thou thy mighty Mass, though altarless,
Offeredst in spirit, and thine offering joined;
And all God's saints on earth, or roused from sleep
Or on the wayside pausing, knelt, the cause
Not knowing; likewise yearned the souls to God
In that fire-clime benign that clears from sin;
And lo! the Lord thy God hath heard thy prayer,
Since fortitude in prayer and this thou know'st'—
Smiling the Bright One spake, 'is that which lays
Man's hand upon God's sceptre. Many a race
Shrivelling in sunshine of its prosperous years
Shall cease from faith, and shamed, though shameless, sink
Back to its native clay; but over thine
God shall extend the shadow of His Hand,
And through the night of centuries teach to her
In woe that song which, when the nations wake,
Shall sound their glad deliverance; nor alone
This nation (Erin) shall to God stand true;
But nations far in undiscovered seas,
Her stately progeny, while ages fleet
Shall wear the kingly ermine of her Faith,
Fleece uncorrupted of the Immaculate Lamb,
For ever: lands remote shall raise to God
Her fanes; and eagle-nurturing isles hold fast
Her hermit cells; thy nation shall not walk
Accordant with the Gentiles of this world,
But as a race elect sustain the Crown
Or bear the Cross: and when the end is come
When in God's Mount the Twelve great Thrones are set
And round it roll the rivers four of fire
And in their circuit meet the peoples three
Of Heaven, and Earth, and Hell, fulfilled that day
Shall be the Saviour's word, what time He stretched
Thy crozier-staff forth from His glory-cloud
And sware to thee, When they that with me walked
Sit with me on their everlasting thrones

Judging the twelve tribes of mine Israel,
Thy people shalt thou judge in righteousness.
Thou, therefore, kneel and bless thy land of Eire.'
Then Patrick knelt, and blessed the land, and said,
'Praise be to God who hears the sinner's prayer.' "

And, being completely satisfied, he added,
"Now, therefore, I will go down from the Rick."

So he descended the slope of Croagh Patrick, and spent Easter joyfully at his dear Aghagower, with Senach the bishop, and his two holy children, Oengus the priest, and the virgin Mathona. Then, with a lighter heart, he resumed his painful missionary journeys.

Each year as Lent began, Patrick was wont to retire into solitude until Eastertide. The particular Lent passed on Croagh Patrick was freighted with more momentous issues than the others, perhaps, on account of the importance of the place in which it occurred. At the very edge of the great Atlantic and on the summit of the lofty cone, Patrick had a pulpit from which he could preach to the men of Ireland for all time; and a pillar reaching heavenward from which to appeal to God for their salvation.

Several places are pointed out as the scenes of his retirement in other years, notably an island in Lough Derg, where his visit is still commemorated in the pilgrimage widely known as "St Patrick's Purgatory." Here in a darksome cave he is said to have passed forty days, seeing many visions of the other world— Heaven, Hell and Purgatory. The cave is now filled up, but the pilgrimage has continued all through the Middle Ages and to our own day; pious pilgrims resorting thither from many lands to spend some time in fasting and prayer, that by this imitation of the Saint, they may obtain his powerful intercession.

Patrick was very strict in the observance of Sunday. Wherever he said the first vespers of that day, he remained without moving forward until tierce on Monday. In this way he provided himself and his clergy with the necessary time and quiet for prayer. Such persons as interrupted the holy silence of the Sabbath by servile work were severely reprimanded; and even if they were pagans or workmen of a pagan king, it was at their peril that they disobeyed his request to cease their toil.

His devotion to the sign of the cross was remarkable. It may indeed be said that in his missionary journeys he signed Ireland with that sacred symbol. Landing in the east he proceeded to the far west; then going to the most northerly point he descended to the south of Munster; and though here he did not quite reach the sea, the cross was formed. Thus the whole land received its own special blessing.

It was his custom, we are told, to make the sign of the cross of Christ over himself a hundred times every day and every night. He traced the sacred sign in the air and demons fled, or wicked men were brought to a standstill in their actions. He signed the earth and it opened to swallow up false gods or evil wizards. He blessed the water with a cross, and it became pure and fit for baptism, even when it had been an object of worship to the heathen; or again, when sprinkled over lifeless creatures, it restored them. It was the sign of the cross that delivered him from the poison in his cup at Tara. No wonder that he paid due honour to the cross wherever he saw it erected as a Christian sign. For, whether he was in a chariot or on horseback, he used to go to every cross, and though it were a mile out of his way he would not pass it by, provided he saw it or knew that it was there.

Now, once, on a certain day, Patrick omitted to visit a cross that was on his road, but he was unaware of its existence and did not see it. The company had reached their halting-place for the night and the Saint was about to sit down to his frugal meal, when the charioteer said to him:

"Thou hast left a cross to-day on thy path without visiting it."

Surely the clerics were angry with the charioteer; for no sooner had Patrick heard his words than he left the guest-house, and his dinner, and went back to the cross.

"This is a grave," said he. "Who hath been buried here?"

Out of the grave the dead man answered:—

"A wretched heathen am I. I was buried here. Whilst I was alive I did evil to my soul, and I fell while doing so, and was buried here."

"What was the cause," said Patrick, "of setting on thy grave the symbol of the Christians, namely, the cross?"

"Not hard to say," answered the voice from the earth. "A certain woman was dwelling in a distant land, and in her absence her son was buried here in this country. And when she returned, she set the cross on this grave. She was unable, through her grief, to recognise the grave of her son."

"That is why I passed the cross," said Patrick, "because it is on the heathen's grave."

And he had the cross removed at once and set up on the grave of the Christian son, whose mother had been so grievously mistaken.

Patrick's veneration for the cross was but the symbol of his love for Christ, of Whom he says:—

> "Christ with me, Christ before me, Christ behind me,
> Christ in me, Christ below me, Christ above me,
> Christ at my right, Christ at my left!
> Christ in the heart of everyone who thinks of me,
> Christ in the mouth of everyone who speaks to me,
> Christ in the eye of everyone who sees me,
> Christ in the ear of everyone who hears me!"

St Patrick was a man of prayer, and a man who added penance and mortification to prayer. Had it not been for this spirit of union with God through Christ all his strenuous labours for the conversion of pagan Ireland would have been empty and fruitless. The magnificent testimony of a whole nation accepting the faith, and keeping it for ever, in spite of every effort of their enemies to wrest it from them, in spite of the "dungeon, fire and sword" of persecutors, is the most powerful proof that can be brought forward of the efficacy of St Patrick's intercession for his beloved people, to whom the poet imagines him saying:—

"Happy Isle!
Be true; for God hath graved on thee His Name,
God, with a wondrous ring, hath wedded thee;
God on a throne divine hath 'stablished thee;
Light of a darkling world! Lamp of the North!
My race, my realm, my great inheritance,
To lesser nations leave inferior crowns;
Speak ye the thing that is; be just, be kind;
Live ye God's Truth, and in its strength be free!"

Chapter VIII

Further Labours in Connaught

T PATRICK pursued his way through Connaught, pausing beside lake, and stream, and spring, to baptize the thousands who flocked to hear his preaching. One day he reached the well of Slan, "The Healer," and heard that it was an object of worship to the pagans. A four-cornered slab of stone closed the square mouth of the well. Under this slab the deluded people believed that a certain dead wizard had been buried in the water at his own request, because he feared the fire and therefore desired that his bones should be always washed by the water. The people worshipped the cooling water and, perhaps, also the dead wizard.

But Patrick was jealous for the glory of the living God, and he rebuked them, saying—

"You speak untruly when you assert that this fountain is king of waters. Raise the stone and see what is under it, whether bones or not, for in my opinion there are no human bones beneath it, though perhaps some gold and silver, but none of your foolish offerings."

There were present a great number of druids and a crowd of people, eager to see what would happen. Some men came forward to remove the stone according to the Saint's command, but they could not by any means get it out of its place. Then Patrick made the sign of the cross over it and said to the people—

"Draw back a little that you may all behold the power of my God Who dwells in heaven—"

And stretching out his hands he moved the stone and placed it above the fountain near its mouth, and, says the chronicler, it is still there. They found nothing in the well but water, and, recognising their folly, they listened to Patrick and believed in the Most High God. Patrick, being weary, sat down on a stone which was placed for him by a youth of the place named Coeta, whom he baptized, and to whom he said—

"Thy posterity shall be for ever blessed."

Innumerable were the signs and wonders wrought by Patrick wherever he went, and no one can reasonably doubt that in him was fulfilled that promise of Our Lord to His Apostles that they should work still greater miracles than those which He Himself had wrought during His mortal life.

A curious story is told of a man long dead who was called forth from his grave by Patrick that he might testify to the power of God. Another prodigy was the assistance given to the charioteer who was in despair of finding the horses when they had gone astray in the darkness of the night. Patrick merely held up his hand with the result that his five fingers, like lamps, threw so brilliant a light over the plain that the missing animals were discovered at once.

Patrick had a nephew called Munis, brother of St Lomman, who came with him to Ireland. Munis had been consecrated bishop and was at his uncle's disposal for any of the new missions he founded. One day when they came to a halting-place, Munis set his crozier upon the branch of a tree, and on leaving the place he forgot to take it with him. In great distress, he made known his loss to the Saint, lamenting and asking leave to go back in search of it. Patrick, smiling, pointed to a branch in front of them, and there lay the crozier, much to the joy of Munis.

"Let thy crozier be mine," said Patrick, "and let this be thine,"—offering his own crozier, not, of course, the Staff of Jesus, to his nephew. So the exchange took place and Munis was glad to obtain the Saint's crozier, which he preserved afterwards as a relic. Munis stood high in his uncle's opinion, as we may infer from the statement that Patrick entrusted a twelfth of Ireland to him to baptize; and he was, apparently, one of the twelve men for whose eternal salvation the Saint interceded on the Rick of Cruachan, one of those of whom he said to the angel—

> "Let them that with me toiled, or in the years
> To come shall toil, building o'er all this land
> The fortress-temple and great house of Christ
> Equalled with me, my name in Erin share."

While Patrick was on the mountain, Munis was on his way to Rome; for news had come to the remote island in the "ultimate parts of the earth," that another "Abbot of Rome" had been elected. This was no less a pontiff than Pope Leo I the Great, and the year was A.D. 441, following that of his election (440). Nothing would have given Patrick greater joy than to make the journey to Rome himself, and to present his homage to the successor of St Peter. But this was out of the question at the present moment. He, therefore, sent Bishop Munis, with letters and a detailed account of his missionary work, asking for the Pope's approval and blessing. Leo's great soul was rejoiced by the news; he treated Munis with great cordiality, gave him a store of most precious relics and sent him back to Patrick with every encouragement and benediction in his power to confer.

When Munis had reached Ireland and was making his way

towards Patrick he stopped for a night at the place afterwards known by the far-famed name of Clonmacnoise. There was no guest house there at this time, so Munis was obliged to sleep in whatever poor shelter he could find. His chief object of anxiety was, however, the casket of precious relics he had brought from Rome. He and his companions thought that the safest place for them would be the interior of a hollow elm tree standing close by their lodging, so in it they placed the casket.

"In this spot," said Munis, "a man of God hath been buried, for a service of angels is therein."

Bishop Munis was right, for, by the side of the hollow elm tree a holy hermit, who went by the name of "Patrick's Leper," had lived and died. The story goes that when the missionaries were about to set sail for Ireland, this good man who was already a leper begged earnestly that they would take him with them. It was not judged expedient to give him a place in their crowded boat; but Patrick, ever compassionate, cast his altar-stone into the sea and told the leper to sit upon it. In this way he was carried in the ship's wake to Ireland. He was called ever afterwards "Patrick's Leper." When the Saint was at Umall, the leper, feeling his end approaching, took up his abode by the hollow elm tree. At first he sat between two branches of the fallen tree, but soon a passer-by came to his aid.

"Art thou a believer?" said the leper.

"Yes," said the man.

"Then," continued the leper, "give me a bundle of those rushes yonder, which thou art taking out by the roots. Give me also in a clean vessel the water which will spring out afterwards."

The man did as requested, and as he was ready to give further help:

"Bring, then, tools for digging the earth," said the leper, "that thou mayst bury me here."

Patrick's leper was the first dead man who was placed under

the clay at Clonmacnoise. And later on the well was called after St Ciaran.

Munis and his companions were stricken with grief in the morning, when, going to the hollow elm tree, they found that during the night it had closed up over their relics. Not knowing whether it would be lawful to break open the miraculous wood, they went on to Patrick, and when the first greetings were over, they told him what had happened.

"A son of life will come there," said the Saint, "and he will require those relics," referring to the great St Ciaran, the founder of Clonmacnoise.

Then Bishop Munis, weary of his travels, asked Patrick to provide him with a fixed diocese.

"My brothers, the bishops Mel and Rioc," he said, "have obtained places."

Though he would have preferred the hillside, he was appointed to Forgney, down by the lake, for, said Patrick:

"The stead below is good rather than the high hill yonder. There will not be many souls going to heaven from the hill, whereas at the ford there will be many."

"It is grievous to me," said Bishop Munis sadly, "to have the lake near me. The warriors, with their shouts and their tumult, will wear out my life."

Patrick was of the same opinion, for the water attracted the people and the soldiers, and there was continual traffic at the ford. The Saint prayed, therefore, and God took the lake out of that place and moved it to a different region. Bishop Munis was provided with all things necessary, including a bronze credence-table, with a pipe of gold which Patrick greatly valued, the crozier before mentioned, relics of SS Peter and Paul, and many others. And having comfortably settled his nephew, our Saint, for whom there was no rest, since all Ireland was his care, went on his way, scattering blessings around him.

When Patrick had crossed the river Moy and entered the district of Tirawley, he saw coming towards him a magnificent train of royal chariots drawn by spirited horses. Twelve princes were driving to Tara to lay a dispute before the High King. They were the sons of King Amalgaid (Awley), who had died, leaving the succession to his throne doubtful, for there were twenty-four ancient tribes in the land, and they had refused to take over them a man with a nickname.

Now the eldest of the brothers, Enda, was surnamed Crom, or The Bent, and for this reason he was not pleasing to the people. The haughtiest and most ambitious of the sons of Amalgaid was Oengus, and he strove to give nicknames to all his brothers, in order that he might be king. He forgot himself so far as to call them "Bare-poll," "One-ear," "Kettle-face," and similar rude epithets.

So the twelve brothers were now hurrying to Tara that a decision might be made by Laeghaire and his brother Eogan, who had been chosen as umpires. When they had sped past the missionaries, Patrick consulted with his clerics as to the advisability of trying to preach in Tirawley in the absence of its chieftains. It was considered by all to be a useless undertaking, for the people would not move without the sanction of authority. Patrick, therefore, turned his chariot towards Tara and followed the princes.

Enda Crom had a son named Conall, a youth of splendid promise, straight as a dart, tall and handsome, brave and generous, with an eloquence beyond his years in defending his father's cause. None of his brothers inspired the crafty Oengus with such fear as this young nephew, for he dreaded the astuteness of the lad in defending his right. When the great gates of Tara were thrown open, therefore, Oengus forbade the doorkeepers to admit Prince Conall. The disappointed boy saw the gates closed, and knew that there was nothing to be done but to wait outside disconsolately for his father.

It happened that Oengus was the foster-son of King Laeghaire, and while all the brothers were cordially welcomed, he met with special honour and affection, so that before the discussion opened it was evident that his claim was likely to win. But Oengus had counted solely on his own efforts and, as often happens, the very precautions he took were the cause of his defeat. If he had admitted his nephew into the fortress he might still have outwitted or overcome so inexperienced a youth.

While Conall was sadly gazing up at the impenetrable walls of Tara, wondering how his father's suit was proceeding, a sound broke upon his ear. It was the ringing of a bell and it came from the direction of the fountain flowing from the side of the hill. This was Patrick's method of drawing the people round him, that they might hear his preaching. Prince Conall went at once to pay homage to the Saint, whose fame had spread throughout the land. Patrick was pleased with the frank, open expression on the boy's face and smilingly blessed him.

Then, as if calling to memory a thing long past, Conall asked the Saint if he could enlighten him as to the meaning of certain words sung by two young girls of Fochlut Wood where he had been fostered. These words were well known and were much talked of in the neighbourhood:

"All the Irish children cry to thee: We beseech thee, holy youth, come and once more walk amongst us!"

"It is I who was called thus," said Patrick; and I heard it when I was biding in the isles of the Tyrrhene Sea. And I know not whether the words were spoken within me or outside me. I will go with thee into thy country, to baptize, to instruct, and to preach the gospel."

While speaking to the young prince, Patrick felt that there was something strange in his being there alone, when he had met him in his father's chariot on the road. To the Saint's inquiry as to the cause of his exclusion from the palace, Conall gave the simple and direct reply that he had not been allowed to enter. It was a case of clear injustice such as Patrick could not endure.

He approached the doors, and at his appearance they were at once thrown open.

"Enter now," said he to Conall, "the doors being open; and go to Eogan, son of Niall, a faithful friend of mine, who will help thee if thou take secretly the finger next his little finger, for this is always a token between us."

The youth did as he was told, and no one opposed his entrance. Approaching Eogan he took his hand in greeting as Patrick had said, and was at once understood.

"Welcome," said Eogan, "what is Patrick's desire?"

"That you should help me," said Conall.

When Prince Conall was allowed his turn to speak before King Laeghaire, he argued thus—

"If, indeed, it be according to age that succession to a palace and lands is decided, I have no right, for I am the youngest. But if it be according to my father's age, then Enda Crom is the eldest of the disputants."

To this Laeghaire answered disapprovingly—

"Verily, speech should be allowed to the oldest and not to the youngest!"

But, influenced, doubtless, by Eogan, he decided that Enda Crom should reign, but that the land should be divided according to justice.

"Howbeit," he added, "if jewels and treasures have been given to any one, they shall not be taken from him."

Now that the dispute was settled, it would be possible for the missionaries to preach in Tirawley. The princes drove off once more in their chariots, followed by Patrick in his, which made the thirteenth. And by the side of the Apostle, by special invitation, was the victorious Prince Conall, pouring out his grateful thanks in eloquent words and promising to do all that he could for the propagation of the faith in the domains which one day would be his own.

But Oengus was wrathful with his brother and nephew, and with Patrick for abetting them, and he made a plot for their destruction. Not content with the intention of staining his own hands with their blood, he endeavoured to gain over his brothers, Fergus and Fedilmid, to be his accomplices in the evil deed. The two princes, however, though they feared to refuse, were averse from committing so grievous a crime as the murder of their own brother and nephew, not to speak of the Saint whose death would draw down the vengeance of heaven. They tried by various devices to evade discussing the question. Fergus pretended to have fallen asleep, but Oengus was not to be imposed upon. Finally, the brothers flatly refused to have anything to do with the wicked project.

"We will not kill the innocent Patrick," they said, "we will not, moreover, commit fratricide upon our brother."

Oengus left to himself, waited until they reached home. Then, taking with him two wizards, Reon and Rechred, and followed by two bands of soldiers, he went openly against Enda and his party. Rechred, the chief druid, was accompanied by nine of his priests, clothed in their ceremonial garments of white. Reon was the more violent of the two, declaring that the earth would open and swallow up Patrick the moment he set eyes upon him. This was a vain boast for which he might have paid the penalty of his own life; for Patrick, on hearing of it from a messenger, said quietly and, it may be, a little grimly—

"Truly it is I who shall first see him."

And we read that the moment the Saint's eyes fell upon the boastful wizard he began to sink slowly into the earth. His courage failed when he found that his magic arts were of no avail, and vainly struggling he cried out in his despair—

"I will believe if I am saved."

At once the earth flung him up to a great height above the winds and when he fell down again he was but half alive. Having learnt his lesson he believed, and was afterwards baptized.

A great multitude was gathered round the well of Crosspatrick for instruction and baptism, and they were witnesses of the miracle. Undaunted by what they supposed to be mere magic, Rechred and his priests pressed on, while Oengus led his men in battle array. But their pride was vanquished when the arch-druid was suddenly thrown up into the air, and falling with great violence his head was broken upon a stone. Fire from heaven consumed his body to ashes, but the "Wizard's Stone" remained as a memorial of his terrible fate, and as a perpetual warning that God is not to be trifled with by proud and ambitious men. The church of Crosspatrick was built there, a little to the east of Fochlut Wood, near the Wizard's Hill, where the troop of the heathen stood.

Oengus was greatly agitated, though not convinced, by these marvels.

"I will believe," he said, "if my sister Fedelm, who died a long time ago, is brought to life."

Patrick saw that it was important to win this powerful prince, at least to an external profession of faith, so that through him he might reach his people. Therefore, taking young Conall with him, he went to the dead woman's grave along the lower path. Oengus and his followers took the same direction along the upper path. Behind flocked an innumerable multitude, some for one side, some for the other.

When the two companies reached the grave, they stood round about it, attentively watching for the issue. Patrick not only raised the woman long dead to life, but also her infant son who had been buried with her. And both were immediately baptized in the well close by, called "One Horn" from the steep little hillock that stands beside it. Then Fedelm, upon whom all eyes were fixed with curiosity mingled with awe, raised her voice and told the multitude about the pains of hell and the rewards of heaven, of which she could speak with the authority of personal experience. With tears she besought her brother Oengus to believe in God through Patrick that so he might secure the salvation of his soul.

Oengus was at last convinced in intellect though his heart was hardened by selfishness and long continued self-indulgence. He believed, and asked for baptism, and with him on that day twelve thousand Tirawley men were baptized in the One Horn well. Seven of the twelve princes were baptized at the same time, the other five or, with Conall, six being doubtless already Christians. The old verse says—

> "In one day they are baptized
> Twice six great thousands,
> Together with Amalgaid's seven sons,
> That was well."

And Patrick left with them one of his best men, Manchen, surnamed the Master, to instruct them further in the faith and to minister to their spiritual needs.

Though the clansmen of Oengus were sincerely converted to Christianity, the chieftain himself had not the courage of his convictions and relapsed almost immediately into his evil habits. To make matters worse he sought to console himself for his disappointment and to drown his remorse for his infidelity to his promises by drinking to excess. His ungraciousness and rudeness towards Patrick went to such extremes as to stand almost alone in the record of the Saint's missionary career.

It had been arranged that Patrick should have a portion of land in the territory of Oengus on which to build a church. A suitable spot was chosen near Lough Dalla and the work was begun. Oengus meanwhile repented of his forced generosity, and, forgetting the respect due to St Patrick and his own dignity as a royal prince, he presented himself one day in a state of semi-intoxication to protest against the building of the church.

The Saint had, perhaps, been more patient with Oengus than with any other sinner in the land. Not only had he forgiven him for attempting to take his life, but he had treated him with the most forbearing and constant kindness. This latest exhibition of depravity disgusted him beyond measure and he broke out into impetuous denunciation.

"By my faith," he said, "it were right that thy dwellings and thy children after thee should not be exalted! Those who succeed thee shall be given to ale-drinking, and they will be wrong doers through thy fault!"

In confirmation of this we are told that the posterity of Oengus followed his example, and, as a consequence, they died out completely in Ireland and their names were heard no more in the annals of the nation.

But Prince Conall was dear to the heart of Patrick, not only for his natural good qualities, but also for the great faith and piety which he showed in spiritual things. If the Saint had proposed the sacerdotal or religious life to the young man he would have found no difficulty in persuading him to make the sacrifice of royal rank, wealth and lands and all the world holds dear. All good men and women, however, were not called upon to enter religion in Patrick's time any more than in our own, though the aspiration towards the highest perfection was then, as now, a common experience.

"The people of Ireland," says Patrick in his "Confession," "who had no knowledge of the true God, but until now always adored false gods and unholy things, how are they now become

St. Patrick marking Connal's Shield with the Cross.

a nation belonging to the Lord and are called the children of God! The sons of the Irish and the daughters of their kings are seen to become monks and virgins of Christ."

"Arise, O Conall," said Patrick one day with some abruptness, "thou must take the crozier."

Without a moment's hesitation the prince answered—

"If it be pleasing to God I will do it for thee."

Greatly rejoiced at the good dispositions of the youth, St Patrick, nevertheless, would not take advantage of a misunderstanding brought about by his ambiguous words—

"That shall not be so," he said, "for God does not call thee to bear the crozier in thy hand as a bishop, but on thy shield as a warrior of Christ. Thou shalt fight in arms for the sake of the heritage of thy people and thy name shall be Conall of the Crozier-Shield. Dignity of laymen and of clerics shall be among thy descendants and in the case of every one of them on whose shield shall be the sign of my crozier, the warriors who follow him shall not be turned to flight."

Aubrey de Vere celebrates this as the inauguration of Irish chivalry—

> " 'Thou shalt not be a priest,' he said;
> 'Christ hath for thee a lowlier task;
> Be thou His soldier! Wear with dread
> His Cross upon thy shield and casque!
> Put on God's armour, faithful knight!
> Mercy with justice, love with law;
> Nor e'er, except for truth and right,
> Thy sword, cross-hilted, dare to draw.'
> He spake and with his crozier pointed
> Graved on the broad shield's brazen boss
> (That hour baptized, confirmed, anointed
> Stood Erin's chivalry) the cross;
> And there was heard a whisper low
> From one unseen—St Michael, thine!
> 'Thou sword, keep pure thy virgin vow,
> And trenchant shalt thou be as mine.' "

Patrick had not lost sight of the prospect opened out by the unexpected words spoken by Prince Conall at their meeting outside the fortress of Tara. The refrain—

"All the Irish children cry unto thee: We beseech thee, holy youth, come once more and walk amongst us, and save us!" was deeply graven on his memory, for it had rung in his ears through all his wanderings. He had not yet set foot in Fochlut Wood, from which those voices seemed chiefly to come, and he was now on the borders of it.

It was not, however, necessary for him to go in search of the dear children of Gleru in their father's hut, for his fame had preceded him and they were already on their way to meet him. The babes of years ago were now grown up women, but they had kept their hearts and souls in all the whiteness of their childhood's innocence for the sake of Patrick's God Who was one day to claim them for His own. Never had they forgotten the holy youth whose teaching had given them their first glimpse of heavenly secrets. In patience and prayer they had awaited his return and now they were exceedingly rewarded.

There was little need of instruction for these heaven-taught virgins; they were ready for baptism and for the immediate reception of the religious veil which Patrick placed upon their heads. A convent with a small church attached to it rose on the neighbouring hillside, and soon they were joined by other consecrated virgins. There they lived in sanctity for the remainder of their lives, remarkable for the heavenly joy which beamed upon their faces; and there they died, singing, as the legend tells, the Magnificat of the Virgin Mother. They were afterwards honoured as the patronesses of the district of Forgland, a name derived from Fochlut.

All who came to St Patrick with faith and confidence experienced the efficacy of his intervention in their behalf. The

St. Patrick met by Virgins in the Wood of Fochlut.

blind and the lame, children and their parents, rich and poor, owed debts to him.

A certain blind man in his eagerness to be cured ran so hastily that a member of Patrick's household was moved to laughter at his stumbling efforts. The Saint was angry at his follower's heartless mirth—

"For thy punishment" he exclaimed, "it were meet that thou shouldst be the blind man."

So the blind man was cured and recovered his sight, while the other was afflicted with blindness to the end of his days.

Again, two lame men came to Patrick to complain that they were practically disinherited by their affliction. This was because part of their land was on high ground and part low, so that they could not attend to it. "Why should we say more?" asks the narrator, as if the miracle were a mere matter of course. "They were heard."

Miracles of this kind were often rewarded by the gift Patrick coveted most—that of land on which to build a church. So, Aed the Tall, being healed of lameness, at the well near Crosspatrick, bestowed that portion of his territory on the Saint. Many also were the druids and wizards who were converted, or who, refusing to listen to the gospel teaching, met with prompt and severe chastisement that their example might serve as a warning to others.

Patrick never allowed an act of courtesy or kindness, even on the part of a child, to go with out some token of gratitude. Some little boys were fishing at a ford in the river Drowes when the Saint was crossing and they did him a small service with good grace. He blessed the water that it might be favourable to them, with so powerful a blessing that ever afterwards even little boys could catch fish in it; and, according to the same story-teller, there was no finer salmon to be caught in all Ireland than that of the river Drowes on account of St Patrick's blessing.

With this passage across the river which separates Leitrim from Donegal, St Patrick's long journeys in Connaught came to an end. His labours there are thus summarised by one chronicler—

"Thrice did Patrick wend across the Shannon into the land of Connaught. Fifty bells, and fifty chalices, and fifty altar-cloths, he left in the land of Connaught, each of them in his church. Seven years was he a-preaching to the men of Connaught. He left a blessing with them and bade them farewell."

Of the toil required for the founding of these fifty missions in a land hitherto unapproached by Christianity we can hardly form an idea. We have seen how he prayed and fasted on special occasions, but we must not forget that his prayer was continual and his ordinary fasting severe. We know, too, that the promise made at Marmoutier never again to touch flesh meat was faithfully kept, so that his abstinence equalled his fasting. It was little wonder that those who studied his life carefully spoke of him in the highest terms of praise and likened him to the greatest servants of God in past times:—

"He was a just man, with purity of nature like the patriarchs. A true pilgrim, like Abraham; gentle and forgiving of heart like Moses; a shrine of wisdom like Solomon; a vessel of election for proclaiming truth like Paul the Apostle; humble and mild towards Sons of Life; gloomy, ungentle, to Sons of Death; a laborious and serviceable slave to Christ; a king for dignity and power, for binding and loosing, for freeing and enslaving, for killing and raising to life."

Yet for all this he was most human; a man weary with labour and longing to lay down the burden and be at rest. But God willed that he should traverse the length as well as the breadth of the island. This was enough for Patrick, who had entirely conformed his will to that of his Divine Master, for Whose dear sake he would have journeyed through the world till doomsday.

Chapter IX

In the North

AVING passed into Ulster, Patrick crossed over the river Erne and found himself in the territory of that Cairbre, son of Niall, who had sought to kill him at Telltown, and whom he had designated as "God's foe." It was a beautiful land, where Christianity might well have found a peaceful home, had it not been for the wickedness of its possessor. No sooner had Cairbre heard of the approach of the missionaries than he ordered two of his warriors—Carbacc and Cuangus—to go and expel them.

Carbacc and Cuangus came, therefore, to Patrick and ordered him to depart from their chieftain's land—

"What you do is not good," remonstrated the Saint, "for if I were permitted to have a dwelling here, my city, with this river running through it, would be a second Rome of Latium with its Tiber; and thy children, O Cairbre, would be my successors therein."

This message was communicated to Cairbre, but he was obstinate in his refusal to allow the preaching of the new faith in his territory. The men returned to drive out the clerics, and

Carbacc set a dog at Patrick. Cuangus, however, disapproving of such violence, beat off the animal with his stick. Meanwhile, Patrick's giant, Bishop MacCartan, was vigilantly on the defensive. But the Saint stood fearless and majestic, leaning upon the Staff of Jesus, while he pronounced the fate of the two warriors. The descendants of both were to be few in number on account of their complicity in the resistance of Cairbre. In the race of Carbacc there would be no dignity, whether of Church or State, but in that of Cuangus, whose behaviour had been more moderate, there would be ordained men. This reward of vocations to the ecclesiastical state, was one upon which high value was always set, and we are told that the family of Cuangus received it while that of Carbacc was deprived of it.

Cairbre had promised to Cuangus that if he expelled the Christians he should have as much land as he could see to the north of where Patrick and his companions stood. They came to the spot for the purpose of settling this question, but, when Cuangus looked to the north, a dark cloud closed round him, so that he could see only a short distance on either hand. This was a disappointment to Cuangus, but Cairbre himself was not to go without his punishment. Patrick sent him this message:—

"The river that God hath given thee, O Cairbre, shall not be fruitful as regards fishing in thy share of it, that is the northern portion, though in the southern part it shall be full of fish."

This prophecy was fulfilled until the time of St Columbcille, when, the northern portion being given to him, it became once more fruitful of fish.

Pursuing a north-easterly course Patrick reached Lough Derg, where, according to tradition, he retired into solitude to spend the forty days of Lent in prayer and fasting. Thus he founded the famous place of pilgrimage whither so many thousands have since then resorted and still continue to resort for the pious purpose of accomplishing "St Patrick's Purgatory." Though there is no written record of this visit of our Saint to Lough Derg, the constant testimony to it and to the efficacy of his intercession is a proof beyond contradiction.

Strengthened and comforted by intimate converse with God, the Apostle once more took to the road, singing, as he went, his favourite praises of the great King of all the elements, ever submissive to the will of the "God of white heaven," and closely united to his dearly loved Christ, Who, as he always said, "worketh with me."

He was now approaching the hereditary domains of his friend Eogan, Son of Niall, with whom he had made the compact at Tara that his messengers should take hold of the finger next the little finger of the prince when they desired his protection. But though Eogan had proved so friendly to Patrick at his brother's court he was not yet a Christian and it was necessary that the missionaries should conduct themselves with great prudence and tact in order not to destroy the good impression which had already been made.

"Beware," said Patrick to his clerics, "lest the lion Eogan, son of Niall, become hostile towards you."

It was, perhaps, at this time that the Saint retired into solitude, for the clerics without Patrick, were advancing cautiously with Sechnall at their head, when they came in sight of Eogan's troops who were guarding his frontiers under the command of his son Muiredach, a noble young warrior who was naturally inclined towards Christianity. Sechnall entered into a parley with the prince whom he found amenable.

"Thou shalt have a reward for it," he said, "if thou canst prevail on thy father to believe."

"What is the reward?" asked Muiredach. "The kingship of thy tribe shall assuredly till doom be given to thee," answered Sechnall.

Muiredach was satisfied with this promise and asked for baptism, which, when properly instructed, he received with good dispositions. In the fresh fervour of his conversion he went to his father and earnestly exhorted him to accept the faith. But Eogan was not easily prevailed upon, and did not return to his own territory while Patrick was there. It was only later that the Saint met him in the Great Wood "where the flagstone is"—and there he believed and was baptized.

"If thou hadst believed in thine own country," said Patrick to him, "hostages of the Gael would have come to thee there; but now hostages will not come, save those thou shalt have by virtue of thy weapons and thy onslaughts."

Eogan was the bravest of warriors but there was something wanting in his personal appearance.

"Not stately am I," he said sadly, "my brothers are greatly shamed by my ugliness."

A foolish story is told that St Patrick worked a miracle to make Eogan as handsome and as tall as he chose to be, but fortunately we are not bound to take this literally; moreover, the meaning is perfectly clear from a spiritual point of view. Baptism certainly worked a miracle in the soul of the grand old pagan, rendering it beautiful and increasing in stature as to heavenly things.

"Which of thy sons is dearest to thee?" asked Patrick of Eogan.

"Muiredach," replied the father.

"Kingship shall descend on him for ever," said Patrick. "And after him?"

"Fergus," said Eogan.

"Ordained priests shall descend from him. And then?"

"Eochu the Tuneful."

"Warriors from him. And after him?"

"All the rest are equally beloved by me," said Eogan.

"Then," said Patrick, "be good to each of them according to his merits."

Eogan invited the missionaries to visit his magnificent fortress at Ailech of the Kings, then second in Ireland only to Tara. The princes and clerics mounted the hill together and the strangers were made welcome to the royal table. Before leaving, Patrick bestowed a blessing of valour on Eogan, and blessed his sons and their land, promising that they should rule right royally and that their enemies would quail before them. He also blessed the fortress, and left his flagstone there, and prophesied that kings and ordained persons out of Ailech would be over Ireland.

Patrick's flagstones are often spoken of by the chronicles. They probably mean the stone altars on which he said Mass, or the consecrated altar-stones which he carried about with him; or again, stones upon which he stood while administering baptism or preaching to the thousands who flocked round him in his triumphal progress through the country. The particular stone at Ailech is supposed to have been the coronation stone of its kings, but there is no certainty on this point.

While still in the neighbourhood of Ailech of the Kings, it came to pass that Patrick retired to pray and left his clerics to preach, baptize and care for the spiritual needs of the multitude. Then there came a chieftain who insisted that his one-eyed son should be ordained priest and even consecrated bishop. Patrick's "strong man" Bishop MacCartan was there present with his brother, and when the chieftain said—

"Confer ye the rank of bishop on my son," MacCartan replied:

"Ask that of Patrick."

But his brother feared to irritate the warrior.

"It is our duty," he said.

This was untrue, for such an ordination was quite contrary

to the canons of the Church. Nevertheless the timorous bishops performed the ceremony of ordination which, as all know, leaves a character upon the soul that can never be effaced. When Patrick was made aware of what had happened in his absence he was extremely angry with the brothers and threatened them and the newly consecrated bishop with punishments for their culpable weakness.

St MacCartan was, notwithstanding, very dear to his master, for he had been his devoted attendant and had helped him lovingly in many a weary journey. His gigantic stature and his enormous physical strength challenged comparison with the smaller and slighter build of St Patrick, but there was no comparison between their powers of endurance. The indefatigable Apostle outlived most of his early friends and worked on courageously when even the strongest of them felt that it was time to give up and take a little ease.

Once, while still in the north, MacCartan as usual took the Saint in his arms to carry him over a difficult place, a task he had often performed with the greatest facility. But this time he put Patrick down with a sigh of relief, exclaiming, "Oh! oh!"

"Indeed," said Patrick, "it is not usual with thee to utter that word."

"I am now an old man, and I am infirm," said Bishop MacCartan, "and thou hast left my comrades in churches, and I am still on the road."

"I will leave thee, then, in a church," said Patrick soothingly. "It shall not be very near, lest we be not good neighbours; nor shall it be very far off, lest we should not be able to visit each other."

So he placed his faithful champion in the episcopal see of Clogher, but there was poverty there, for this was to be MacCartan's punishment for consecrating the one-eyed bishop Echu. And in his brother's see there was always contention;

while Echu's chastisement consisted in his bones not being left in peace.

A certain Bishop Olcan who belonged to Patrick's train of clerics is now presented to us as the subject of a picturesque anecdote, in which the Saint figures as a severe judge. He told Olcan to go forward with his axe upon his shoulder and to fix his abode in the spot where the axe should drop off. In this vicinity there lived a chieftain called Saran, who, for rudely expelling the missionaries from his lands, had been excommunicated by Patrick. Saran was therefore said to be "deprived of heaven and earth," and he certainly deserved chastisement on account of the injustice and cruelty with which he carried off men from other districts and kept them in bondage.

One day, as Saran was dragging some poor wretches into thraldom, Bishop Olcan chanced to be passing by, and the prisoners cried out to him to have pity on them. Olcan begged that they might be set at liberty, but Saran refused to grant the request, except on the condition that heaven should be granted to him.

"Verily," said Olcan, "I cannot do that, since Patrick hath taken it from thee."

"Then," said Saran fiercely, "I will slay thy people about thee, save thee alone, and all these captives shall be slain. And in every place in which I can find a tonsured man, I will put them all under a sword's mouth."

Alarmed at these ferocious threats Bishop Olcan forgot that he could depend on God and Patrick for protection. He was, therefore, so weak as to promise the reversal of Patrick's sentence of excommunication. Saran, assured of heaven in spite of his evil deeds, and with no intention of amending his life, went away, boasting of his victory. Olcan's conscience at once smote him with remorse, and he hastened to ask for forgiveness. According to the somewhat improbable story

Patrick was inexorable. He was driving in his chariot when the repentant bishop met him and knelt down humbly by the roadside.

"Drive the chariot over him," said Patrick, doubtless meaning that Olcan should see to his own safety, but that he would not stop to parley with him.

The charioteer, taking the command literally, was unwilling to obey.

"I dare not make it go over a bishop," he said.

Then Patrick pronounced the sentence of Bishop Olcan, that the chastisement of his weakness might deter others from giving way before tyranny and oppression. His cloister would not be high on earth, and three evils should come to it, namely decay, bloodshed and fire, the two last being fulfilled by the slaughter of the monks by one king, and the burning of the monastery by another.

"And thy land," added Patrick, "shall belong to the little boy who is carrying thy box"—and this also was accomplished.

Saran was the black sheep out of a family of twelve brothers. The other eleven received blessings for their humble acceptance of the true faith and for the generosity with which they fulfilled the obligations it imposed upon them. One of them came forward with a gift of land—

"Thou shalt have from me," he said, "the site of a church."

"In what place dost thou give it to me?" asked Patrick.

"On the bank of the River Bann, in the west," replied the prince, "in that place yonder where the children are burning the fern."

"It shall be mine," said Patrick, "and one day thy grandson shall be its bishop."

The Saint having journeyed eastward along the northern coast of Ireland as far as Fair Head in Antrim, turned southward and reached once more the neighbourhood of Mount Slemish.

Here he found his old friend Bishop Guasacht, son of Milcho, who was faithfully labouring in the vineyard of the Lord, and whom he took with him in his journey southwards. Here also were the holy sisters of Guasacht, known as the two Emers, who had received the religious veil from Patrick and who were living happily in their peaceful convent.

At Findabur he wished to build a cloister, for it seemed to him a convenient spot between the lake and the mountain— that is, Lough Neagh and Slieve Gallion. But Cairthenn the Great, king of that part of the country, came in person to drive out the Christians. So Patrick took his kingship away from him and his descendants and gave it to Cairthenn the Little, who was in exile on account of his brother's tyranny. Cairthenn the Little came to Patrick with his wife to be baptized and blessed in the possession of their new kingdom.

The Saint blessed also their infant daughter, Trea, with a special benediction of virginity and consecration to God—

"This child," he said "will be full of the grace of God, and it is I that shall bless the veil on her head."

It was done as he foretold when Trea was old enough to enter a convent. The story tells prettily how the angels themselves brought her veil down from heaven and set it on her head that Patrick might bless it. But the angelic spirits were not content with covering the young virgin's beautiful hair; they brought the veil so low that her eyes also were concealed. This seemed to Patrick a mistake, so he began to draw the veil higher.

"Why," said the saintly maiden, "is it not good that it should bide as it was placed?"

"Good, indeed, then," said Patrick approvingly, delighted to perceive Trea's love of a hidden life. And during her whole career she saw nothing except so far as she was able to behold earthly things through the angels' veil.

From the shores of Lough Neagh Patrick pressed on westward

till he came to Clogher, of which MacCartan was now bishop. The Saint had not engaged another "strong man" because he was becoming less vigorous with advancing years, and felt the need of a chariot for even his shorter journeys. With the prestige of his wonderful success and with the enthusiasm inspired by his venerable personality he was dispensed from going to find the people. Without waiting to hear the ringing of his bell the multitudes flocked round him, eager to listen to his words and ready to be baptized if they were not yet Christians.

There was near Clogher a most beautiful site sacred from time immemorial to druidical worship. It was an ideal spot for an open-air church where thousands could assemble for divine worship. A natural pulpit was there in the rock, and near it was a large flat block of stone forming an altar on which to celebrate Mass. Here Patrick spent three days and three nights, preaching to the people and baptizing them in the fountains of clear water close at hand.

St Brigid was present, and, being still very young, fell asleep during the preaching. Those around her wished to awaken her, but Patrick would not allow her to be disturbed. When she awoke of her own accord the Saint asked her what she had seen in her dream. The girl answered—

"I saw assemblies of white-clad men, and light-coloured oxen, and white cornfields; speckled oxen behind them and black oxen after these. Afterwards I saw sheep; and dogs and swine and wolves quarrelling with each other. Thereafter I saw two stones, one small and the other large; a shower dropped on them both. The little stone increased at the shower, and silvery sparks would break forth from it. The large stone, however, wasted away."

"Those," said Patrick, "are the two sons of Echaid."

They were Cairbre and Bressal, one of whom believed in God, the other not. Besides giving this explanation of the two stones,

The Vision of the Synod of Clerics.

Patrick expounded the vision of Brigid in a wonderful manner, of which application can be easily made as typical of the stages of the progress of the Church in Ireland: the glorious centuries following on the whole-hearted reception of Christianity; the troubled times to come; with the black persecution and the invasion of quarrelsome heretics, devastating the fold of Christ and devouring His unhappy flock. The portrait is true to life, and there can be no suspicion of making up a prophecy after the event, since the manuscript of the Tripartite Life of Patrick in which it is recorded was written in the bright days preceding the sorrows of later centuries.

The brothers, Cairbre and Bressal, signified by the stones in Brigid's dream, had a sister, the Princess Cinnu, whom her father, King Echaid, dearly loved. The high rank, great beauty, and ample dowry of this noble maiden brought many princes to her father's court with the hope of winning her in marriage. When Cinnu was of marriageable age King Echaid fixed his choice on a grandson of Niall the Great and entered into negotiations with the powerful family with which he hoped to form this alliance, so desirable from every point of view.

Meanwhile the Princess Cinnu was residing in her father's house near Clogher, where Patrick was preaching. One day while walking with her maidens she met the train of missionaries and stopped to listen to Patrick's instructions. The doctrines of Christianity at once appealed to her heart so forcibly that all her thoughts were fixed for ever on the God who cleansed her soul in the waters of baptism. Her fervour was so great that Patrick exhorted her to unite herself to the spiritual Spouse rather than to descend once more to earthly thoughts.

A few days later she came to the Saint to tell him that she had received an inspiration, confirming his words and urging her to become a virgin of Christ in order that she might be nearer to God.

"Deo gratias!" says Patrick in his "Confession," "six days later she realised her divine vocation, giving herself most piously and zealously to God, like so many other virgins of God, who follow the same course not with the goodwill of their parents but rather suffering reproaches and ill-treatment from them."

Echaid, though an unbaptized pagan, had too much respect for Patrick to make violent opposition to his wishes. Cinnu, therefore, asked the Saint to go with her and facilitate the disclosure to her father. The king had just returned from the country of the husband he intended for her, where he had been making arrangements for the marriage. He was seeking her in order to communicate the news when she stood before him arrayed in the white garments of her baptism and wearing on her head the veil of virginity. Patrick was with her and lost no time in coming to the point at issue. The Eternal Spouse had called the maiden and chosen her for His own; there must be no further question of an earthly alliance.

King Echaid was not so rash as to refuse the Saint's request. He agreed, therefore, to give his daughter to God provided that Patrick gave him heaven in exchange, without the condition of baptism. Perhaps the wily king thought that Patrick would not consent to this bargain; and indeed it was a point not easy to settle. We may give his answer in de Vere's words:

> "Then Patrick, on whose face the princess bent
> The supplication softly strong of eyes
> Like planets seen through mist, Eochaid's heart
> Knowing, which miracles had hardened more,
> Made answer, 'King, a man of jests art thou,
> Claiming free range in heaven, and yet its gate
> Thyself close barring! In thy daughter's prayers
> Belike thou trustest, that where others creep
> Thou shalt its golden bastions over-fly.
> Far otherwise than in the way thou weet'st
> That daughter's prayers shall speed thee. With thy word
> I close, that word to frustrate. God be with thee!

Thou living, I return not. Fare thee well!'
Thus speaking, by the hand he took the maid,
And led her through the concourse. At her feet
The poor fell low, kissing her garment's hem,
And many brought their gifts, and all their prayers.
Years came and went, yet neither chance nor change
Might from Eochaid charm his wayward will,
Nor reasonings from the wise that still preferred
Safe port to victory's prize. But far away
Within that lonely convent tower from her
Who prayed for ever, mightier rose the prayer."

At last after many years of stubborn resistance to grace, Echaid felt that his end was drawing near. When about to breathe his last, he said to the friends who surrounded his bed—

"Bury me not until Patrick shall come." With these words on his lips he gave up the ghost.

> "Three days
> The lamentation sounded on the hills
> While by the bier the yellow tapers stood,
> And on the right side knelt Eochaid's son,
> Behind him all the chieftains cloaked in black,
> And on his left his daughter knelt, the nun,
> Behind her all her sisterhood, white veiled,
> Like tombstones after snowstorm."

Though at a great distance, Patrick, on hearing the news of Echaid's death, at once set out and reached the royal fort after a journey of twenty-four hours. The place was full of people mourning and lamenting, and the keeners' plaintive wail could be heard afar off. Patrick ordered all to leave the death chamber, and then, bending his knees to the Lord and shedding abundant tears, he prayed earnestly. After this he said in a loud, clear voice:

"O King Echaid, in the name of Almighty God, arise!"

Straightway, at the voice of God's servant, the king arose, and Patrick threw open the door of the chamber that the people might enter. When Echaid had steadied himself and sat down, he spoke of his wonderful experience in so convincing a manner that the weeping and wailing of the people was turned into joy at the revelation of eternal truths. Then holy Patrick instructed the king in the method of the faith, and baptized him, for Echaid had doubtless by this time realised that no unbaptized soul can enter heaven.

And Patrick commanded him to set forth before the people the punishments of the ungodly and the blessedness of the Saints, and also to preach to the common people that all things made known to them of the pains of hell and of the joys of the blessed who have obeyed, are true. And Echaid preached of both these things as he had been ordered to do. Then Patrick gave him his choice between fifteen years of the sovereignty of his country, if he would live quietly and justly, or going forthwith to heaven if this seemed better to him. But the king at once said—

"Though the kingship of the whole earth should be given to me, and though I should live for many years, I should count it as nothing in comparison to the blessedness that hath been revealed to me. Wherefore I choose more and more that I may be saved from the sorrows of the present world, and that I may return to the everlasting joys that have been shown to me."

Patrick said to him: "Go in peace and depart unto God."

Echaid gave thanks to God in the presence of his household and he commended his soul to God and to Patrick, and sent forth his spirit to heaven. Thus did the Saint accomplish his difficult promise, for Echaid, without being baptized, saw what heaven was, with the result that on returning to life he desired nothing so much as to receive the Sacrament of regeneration.

> "That night nigh sped,
> Two vestals, gliding past like moonlight gleams,
> Conversed: one said, 'His daughter's prayer prevailed!'

The second: 'Who may know the ways of God?
For this, may many a heart one day rejoice
In hope! For this, the gift to many a man
Exceed the promise; Faith's invisible germ
Quickened with parting breath; and baptism given,
It may be, by an angel's hand unseen!' "

Chapter X

From North to South

EAVING the vicinity of Clogher, Patrick pursued an almost direct course towards the south, for his presence near Tara was necessary. It may have been remarked in the course of this history, that the amiable youth, Benignus, who was so dear to Patrick, vanishes completely out of sight during the great missionary journeys of his master. But he was not idle. His studies were early completed, and he was ordained priest, but he was kept at Tara in the post of secretary to the commission of nine distinguished men engaged upon the Christianisation of the Brehon Laws.

This was a work of immense importance undertaken by St Patrick with the reluctant consent of King Laeghaire. The Brehon Laws were admirable and perfectly adapted to the character of the people for whom they had been drawn up. They naturally contained, however, many sections relating to druidical and superstitious usages, and articles enjoining hatred and ill-treatment of enemies directly opposed to Christian charity and humility. The commission consisted of three bishops, of whom St Patrick was the chief; three kings with Laeghaire himself at their head; and three poets, with Dubthach, the King-poet of Erin, as first in rank. It was to be expected, therefore, that, after his long absence in the west and north, Patrick should find it advisable to visit Tara.

We have no record of the Saint's visit to the royal fort, but he remained for a considerable time in the neighbourhood, going further south and returning, before proceeding to Munster, which he now intended to evangelize. There are very few incidents of sufficient interest to detain us here— only the monotonous though most glorious labours of founding churches, monasteries and convents, preaching and baptizing thousands; ordaining and consecrating priests and bishops; healing the sick, consoling the afflicted, blessing men of good- will, and threatening God's judgments on evil-doers. The work was incessant, but its result was the thorough conversion of the entire nation.

It will be remembered that at Patrick's first visit to Tara on the memorable Easter Sunday of the year 433, no one rose up to do him honour in the house save only Dubthach, King-poet of the island of Ireland, and of King Laeghaire; and a stripling of his household named Fiacc. Many years had passed since then and Dubthach had grown old, though he was still revered for his wisdom and had not yet laid aside his harp. He was a fervent and faithful Christian, and between him and Patrick there existed a strong friendship.

Nor had young Fiacc belied the promise of his early days. He was looked upon as a worthy successor to Dubthach in the position of chief bard, and was employed by his master in the customary journeys through the land which Dubthach was now too feeble to undertake in person. Fiacc was married, and his son was being educated in all the bardic lore of Ireland, that he might one day take his father's place.

Now, when Patrick was at Tara about this time, he was much concerned about the appointment of a suitable bishop for the district, which, on account of its constant communication with the rest of the country, as the seat of the High King, required a man of special training and prudence.

The Saint consulted Dubthach on the subject, telling him that the bishop he sought should be young, of comely aspect and well-born; if married, a man of one wife and having only one child. The description applied so exactly to Fiacc that Dubthach was struck with consternation.

"Verily," said he, "this is most unfortunate for me, for Fiacc, son of Erc, is the man you seek. But at present he is gone from me into the lands of the Connaught men, with bardism for the kings."

Dubthach spoke with noble simplicity, making no attempt to hide the fitness of his disciple for an office incompatible with the profession of poet, for which he had been so carefully educated. It would be a difficult task to place the matter before Fiacc in such a way as to ensure his consent to the proposal. Both Patrick and Dubthach shrank from asking Fiacc to give up all his worldly prospects, and even his domestic happiness, though in so good a cause.

Through "Dubthach's cleverness" the problem was solved. The old master knew how dear he was to his disciple, and that Fiacc would be willing to offer himself as a substitute for him in any extremity. He therefore proposed that when Fiacc returned they should try him in the following manner. Patrick would appear to have accepted Dubthach for the clerical order, and would be prepared to tonsure him. They had hardly come to this decision when Fiacc's arrival was announced. All was put in order as it had been settled. When Fiacc entered, he exclaimed in astonishment:

"What is proposed to thee, O master?"

"To make a bishop of Dubthach," said the bystanders.

"Verily this will be a blemish on the common wealth," said Fiacc, "for Ireland has no poet to compare with him, and if he is tonsured, he must abandon his bardism and all the honour attached to it. It is a grief to me that I am not taken in his place."

"Truly thou shalt be taken," was the instant rejoinder of Patrick.

"That is well," replied Fiacc, "for I shall be a much smaller loss to the order of bards, and to Ireland."

Thereupon Fiacc was tonsured, and the necessary books were given to him that he might study the office of the church. And great grace came upon him, so that in an incredibly short space of time he was able to read the ordo of the Mass and the psalms. He was consecrated bishop, and the episcopal see of Leinster was given to him. Moreover, his only son, Fiachra, was ordained priest.

Patrick gave to Bishop Fiacc a complete set of altar requisites with a bell, a credence-table, a crozier, and tablets or altar cards. In order that he might not want help or instruction after his hurried ordination, the Saint left with him seven ecclesiastics of his own household to assist him in the government of his diocese. There was a cloister with a community of monks attached to Fiacc's church, but its situation seems to have been insalubrious, as the following story shows.

When three score the monks had died, an angel appeared to Fiacc in his church and bade him move from that place to the west of the river Barrow. He was to set up the refectory, or monastery, on the spot where he should find a boar, and the church was to be built where a doe was found. But Fiacc very properly refused to do the bidding of the angel until he should have further orders from his primate. St Patrick, hearing of the case, came to Bishop Fiacc; and the places on the west of the river being found according to the indications of the angel, the church and monastery were built and afterwards consecrated and blessed by the Saint. The prince of the district generously gave all the land required for the new foundations.

While still in Leinster Patrick was once quietly praying, according to his custom on a Sunday afternoon, when he heard sounds of labour. On inquiring, he found that a body of workmen were digging the foundations of a royal rath near by. Patrick sent to have the work stopped, but no notice was taken of his message. Indignant at this wilful profanation of the Lord's Day, he foretold that the building would be unstable unless Mass were said there every day. Moreover, the portion of the stronghold set up on Sunday would have to be rebuilt before it could be inhabited.

Many were the churches and monasteries that Patrick founded in Leinster, and going forth from the kingdom he left his blessing with its inhabitants. Then, entering Ossory, he founded churches and cloisters there. He said of the men of Ossory, that they and their descendants should be distinguished in Church and State, and that no other province should prevail over them as long as they were obedient to his instructions. After this, Patrick bade them farewell, and he left with them "relics of ancient holy men," and a party of his household to confirm them in the faith. And even in the present twentieth century it is said that no other part of Ireland gives so many priests to the Church as Ossory.

Having entered Munster, Patrick directed his course towards Cashel of the Kings; and late one night his party pitched their tents at the gates of the royal palace. The arrival of the missionaries was unknown to the sleeping inhabitants, but it made great stir among the sleepless demons who dwelt in the stone idols standing round the courtyard. When Prince

Aengus rose in the morning and went out of doors, he found every one of his father's false gods lying prostrate on the ground, overthrown and vanquished by Christ, the Son of the One, True and Living God.

Aengus does not appear to have been particularly astonished or annoyed at this event, for the idolatrous superstitions of the druids and wizards had by this time been thoroughly discredited in the land. The people of Munster, with their princes, had long been impatiently waiting for the good tidings of Christianity, and they had no further use for their idols. The gates of the fortress were, therefore, thrown open to the missionaries, who were cordially welcomed and bade to enter. The prince conducted Patrick to the spot where his flagstone afterwards stood as a memorial of his blessed presence, and where he is said to have plucked the shamrock of immortal memory.

Aengus and his royal brothers listened with devout attention to the Saint's preaching and asked for baptism. While the ceremony of immersion was proceeding, Aengus stood next to Patrick who inadvertently sent the spike of his crozier through the prince's foot. The young man made no sign, but stood there heroically bearing the pain for the sake of the Crucified Lord who had just cleansed his soul by baptism in His Precious Blood.

"Why didst thou not tell this to me?" cried Patrick in dismay when he saw what he had done.

"It seemed to me," said Aengus simply, "that it was a rite of the faith."

"Thou shalt have its reward," said Patrick, "thy posterity shall not die of a wound from this day for ever."

But the chronicler adds that no one is king of Cashel until Patrick's successor instals him, and confers ecclesiastical rank upon him.

While Patrick was preaching near the fortress of Cashel a man named Ailill withstood him. At that moment the wife of Ailill came up the hill with the terrible news that a boar had killed and practically devoured their little son. The father in his grief said to Patrick:

"I will believe if thou wilt bring my son to life again for me."

Patrick ordered the bones of the child to be gathered together and brought to him. When this was done, he directed Malach the Briton, a cleric of his household, to bring the boy back to life. Malach, however, seized with a temptation of disbelief, said:

"I will not tempt the Lord."

"Sad is that, O Malach!" exclaimed the Saint. "Thy cloister will not be lofty on earth. Thy house will be the house of one man.

Thus it came to pass; for Malach's cloister was so narrow and its land was so poor, that five cows could with difficulty find pasture there. After this failure—

> "The Apostle turned
> To Ibair and to Ailbé, bishops twain,
> And bade them raise the child. They heard and knelt,
> And Patrick knelt between them; and these three
> Upheaved a wondrous strength of prayer, and lo!
> All pale, yet shining, rose the child, and sat,
> Lifting small hands, and preached to those around."

So convincing were the little boy's words that his father and mother believed and were baptized, and all their tribe followed their example. It was on this occasion that Patrick said:

"God heals by the physician's hand," thus disclaiming for himself the honour of the miracle.

Nowhere, perhaps, in all Ireland did Patrick meet with a warmer or more truly royal reception than in Munster, where his coming had been so eagerly desired. His journey through the province was a triumphal progress. He did not, however, go as far as its south and west shores, for he was growing old and his strength no longer sufficed for long and toilsome marches. But the Munster men were not to be deprived of the sight of their great Apostle. They left their distant homes and flocked to hear him, some even taking to their boats and coasting the island until they came near enough to reach him easily by land. He baptized these fervent converts and bestowed special blessings on them and on their families, and lands, on account of the willingness with which they came to him bringing him abundance of gifts. There were as usual some exceptions to the general rule.

A certain Derball opposed him saying:—

"If thou wouldst remove the mountain there in front of us, so that I might see over it the lake which lies to the south, I would believe."

At the prayer of Patrick the mountain began to melt away, but the incredulous Derball, afraid of being obliged to keep his promise, hastily cried out:—

"Though thou do it, thou shalt get nothing for it."

At which Patrick threatened him saying:—

"There shall not till doom be either king or bishop of thy race; and the men of Munster every seventh year shall peel thee and thy successors like an onion."

Again, the Saint had to wait for King Fergair to come to him. This was not customary and showed a want of respect which might have evil consequences.

"Thou hast come slowly," said the Saint severely.

Fergair excused himself saying, "The road is very stiff."

"True, indeed," rejoined Patrick, "there shall never be a king descended from thee."

Knowing that this was not the real reason of his tardy arrival, Patrick questioned Fergair further—

"What was it that delayed thee to-day?"

"Rain delayed us," said the king, still bent on excusing himself.

"Thy people's assemblies shall always take place in showery weather," commented Patrick.

And ever afterwards the assemblies of those people were held at night, probably from some superstitious hope of escaping the punishment.

It is abundantly evident from such stories as these that St Patrick would take no excuse for want of generosity or promptness in the service of God. His right hand was always raised to bless fervour, but his left hand to rebuke and punish the lukewarm and all who sought to shirk their obligations.

After he had founded churches and monasteries in Munster, and ordained clerics of every grade, and healed all manner of diseases, and raised the dead to life, he bade the Munster men farewell and left a blessing with them. Turning his chariot towards the north, and, accompanied by his household, he departed leaving the multitude sorrowfully gazing after them.

When the holy company had disappeared from sight a great longing came over the people to behold once more the face of the Apostle who had drawn their hearts so strongly to himself. The chieftains mounted their horses and eagerly followed the traces of Patrick's chariot-wheels, each vying with the other that he might outstrip him. Their households followed them, and lastly came the great multitude of the common people. And when all these men, women and children overtook Patrick and cast their eyes upon his saintly figure, they raised their voices in joy and uttered a great cry for very gladness of looking upon him again. And the place was for this reason thereafter called Brosnacha or the "Joyful Clamour." After doing further signs and wonders, Patrick bade another farewell to the men of Munster and bestowed yet another blessing upon them saying—

THE people who sat in darkness saw a great light, and they who were in the land and in the shadow of death received light by which came their illumination.

"Blessing on the men of Munster
Girls, boys and women!
Blessing on the land
That gives them fruit.
Blessing on every treasure
That shall be produced on their plains
Without anyone being in want of help,
God's blessing on Munster!
Blessing on their peaks
On their bare flagstones,
Blessing on their glens
Blessing on their ridges.
Like sand of sea under ships,
Be the number of their hearths;
On slopes, on plains,
On mountains, on peaks."

Aubrey de Vere paraphrases the crude literal rendering of this blessing thus:

" 'The Blessing fall upon the pasture broad,
On fruitful mead, and every corn-clad hill,
And woodland rich with flowers that children love;
Unnumbered be the homesteads and the hearths:
A blessing on the women, and the men,
On youth, on maiden, and the suckling-babe:
A blessing on the fruit-bestowing tree,
And foodful river tide. Be true; be pure,
Not living from below, but from above,
As men that overtop the world. And raise
Here, on this rock, high place of idols once,
A kingly church to God. The same shall stand
For aye, or, wrecked, from ruin rise restored,
His witness till He cometh. Over Eire
The Blessing speed, till time shall be no more,
From Cashel of the Kings.'
            The Saint fared forth:
The people bare him through their kingdom broad
With banner and with song; but o'er its bound
The women of that people followed still
A half-day's journey with lamenting voice,
Then silent knelt, lifting their babes on high;
And, crowned with twofold blessing, home returned."

Patrick had now traversed the whole island in all its divisions and kingdoms, and he might consider his missionary journeyings closed by the magnificent display of faith and enthusiasm at Cashel and Brosnacha. It only remained for him to found his primatial See and to consolidate the results of his unremitting toil throughout the years from the day when, as Rome's delegate, he first set foot upon the eastern shore of Ireland. Slowly but surely he had worked his way westward until he stood upon Croagh Patrick; then northwards to the extreme edge of the rocky coast of Antrim, and again south to Cashel and below it; thus signing the whole land with the sacred sign of the cross, which was so dear to his apostolic heart.

Chapter XI

To Armagh and Rest

"PATRICK," says Professor Bury, "did three things. He organised the Christianity which already existed; he converted kingdoms which were still pagan, especially in the west; and he brought Ireland into connection with the Church of the Empire, and made it formally part of universal Christendom. "The church he had founded was in a flourishing condition and full of fervour. But Patrick was now an old man, spent with labours, ready to lay down the burden whenever it should be the will of God.

He was not to die, however, until he had settled in his own primatial See, there to complete and unify his great work. He who had consecrated so many bishops, giving to each a church and a diocese, might at least spend the last years of his life in the administration of a church of his own.

On his northward journey he came once more to the territory of Mag Slecht, where he had overthrown the great stone idol with its twelve minor gods. Foilge, the chieftain of this place, boasted that whenever he met Patrick he would kill him, in vengeance for the destruction of his idols. This boast was known to the men of Patrick's household but they concealed it from the Saint, hoping to be able to frustrate the designs of Foilge. One day Patrick's charioteer, Odran, said to him:—

"Since I am now a long time charioteering for thee, O Master Patrick, let me to-day sit in the chief seat and do thou be charioteer."

It was an unheard-of request and might well have met with a rebuke, but Patrick in all his relations with his household was gentle and simple as a child, ready to comply with their wishes in all things where there was no offence against God.

The lumbering, noisy vehicle was drawn by oxen and in it were two seats, one of honour for the master at the left-hand side, the lower one at the right being for the driver. Odran, therefore, with an appearance of great arrogance, took possession of Patrick's seat, while the Saint sat on his right guiding the oxen. Foilge was in ambush at a convenient spot and presently rushed out, spear in hand. Taking Odran for his master, the chieftain struck a furious blow and the faithful charioteer fell wounded to death.

The story goes on to say that Patrick would have placed Foilge under a ban for this impious deed, but that Odran begged him to turn his anathema against a tree growing by the wayside.

Be it so, then," said Patrick, edified by his servant's forgiveness of injuries. But the chronicler shows no mercy, for he adds— "and Foilge died at once and went to hell." Nevertheless, Patrick blessed the wicked man's son at the request of his mother, and his children held the land.

Further north, the Saint noticed some slaves who were busily engaged in felling a tree. He went towards them for the purpose of finding out whether they had yet received the good tidings of the Gospel. Seeing their hands lacerated and covered with blood, he had compassion on them and asked them who they were.

"We are slaves to Trian," they replied, "in bondage and in great tribulation, and we are not allowed even to sharpen our axes against a flagstone, lest our fate should be less cruel and our task easier. Wherefore blood comes through our hands."

Patrick was touched to the heart, for he knew what it was to suffer in bondage even under a kind master, and his sympathies were always with the unhappy and the oppressed. As a first step towards the relief of the unfortunate slaves he blessed their axes, which forthwith became sharp, and cut properly. Leaving them consoled and encouraged, he went to the king's rath and asked for an interview with Trian.

The heartless employer took little account of his bondsmen's sufferings, or rather, since they were captives taken in battle, he heaped injuries upon them. He would not listen to Patrick's remonstrances, even though the Saint sat at his gate and "fasted against him," refusing to accept of his hospitality unless justice was done to the slaves. Seeing his obduracy, Patrick turned away the next day to continue his journey, saying that of Trian's posterity there would be neither king nor prince, though he was the grandson of King Amalgaid.

"And he himself," added Patrick—sorrowfully confessing his inability to touch that hardened heart—"shall perish early and shall go down into bitter hell."

The prophecy was soon fulfilled. Trian was enraged when he found that it was the slaves who had made known his inhuman conduct to Patrick. He swore to add to their sufferings a hundred fold, and mounted his chariot with the intention of going to bind and beat them himself. But the horses became unmanageable and ran into the lake, dragging the king and his charioteer from their seats. They were drowned, and the lake was named after Trian.

"That was his last fall," says the chronicler grimly, "he will not come out of that lake until the vespers of doomsday, and it will not be for his happiness even then."

Trian's wife did not, however, share in her husband's crimes or in his condemnation. She came to Patrick in deep sorrow and fell on her knees at his feet. He received her with great compassion and kindness, giving her his blessing. He also blessed her children, the eldest son being baptized by Sechnall and the youngest by Patrick himself.

The ancient chroniclers give so many instances of Patrick's severity towards evil-doers that they seem inclined to forget the mild and gentle side of his character. The incorrigible sinner, Trian, was punished as he well deserved for his barbarity and became an example to hard task-masters. But Patrick was all mercy and pity for the poor slaves, and for the oppressed people, and did everything he could for their relief. Another occasion for the prompt execution of justice soon presented itself.

There dwelt at that time in the land of Ulster a certain wicked man named MacCuill. He was impious and a "son of death," violent, treacherous and cruel, constantly descending with his band of robbers from their mountain stronghold to plunder strangers and to slay the faithful. One day Patrick and his companions had to pass through the valley which lay below MacCuill's fortress. The brigand was on the watch and he determined to slay the Saint.

"This," said he to his followers, "is the tonsured man and the falsifier who is deceiving every one. Let us go and make an attack upon him and we shall see whether his God will help him."

The fame of Patrick's miracles had reached them, but they mocked at the reports of his raising the dead and curing the sick, setting these things down to magic. MacCuill decided that before killing Patrick they would amuse themselves by requiring him to work an apparent miracle which would have the effect of turning him into ridicule. One of their number, therefore, was placed upon a bier as if he were dead and the supposed corpse was covered with a mantle. The robbers approached Patrick in solemn procession.

Heal for us our comrade," they said deceitfully, "and make prayer to the Lord that He may raise him to life out of death. "

Patrick calmly answered—

"It would not seem strange to me even if he were dead."

Now Garvan was the man's name, and of him Patrick spoke the words—

> "Garvan's mantle
> Shall be on the body of a corpse,
> But I will declare to you more!
> It is Garvan who shall be under it."

Thoroughly alarmed for the fate of their comrade they began to fear that their trifling was about to bring serious consequences upon them. Taking the mantle from his face they found that the man was really dead. Then they were struck silent with remorse and astonishment, until one of them broke out with the exclamation—

"Truly this Patrick is a man of God!"

They all believed from that moment and even MacCuill believed and was willing to atone for his crimes. Patrick seeing their changed dispositions turned to their leader and asked him with gentle reproach—

"Why didst thou seek to tempt me?"

With heartfelt sorrow MacCuill replied—

"I repent of my evil deed. I am ready to do whatever you command me and I yield myself up to the great God Whom you preach."

Then Patrick instructed them, and to MacCuill he said—

"Believe in my God and in Jesus Christ our Lord. Confess thy sins and be baptized in the name of the Father and of the Son and of the Holy Ghost."

Death of an Imposter.

No sacrifice was too great for the fervent convert whose eyes had been thus instantaneously opened to divine things. He acknowledged that it had been his intention to kill Patrick and he begged the Saint to impose a heavy penance upon him for the crime. But Patrick refused to be his judge. "No," he said, "it is not I but God who will judge thee."

MacCuill made a public confession of all his wickedness, expressed his sincere belief in the doctrines of Christianity and received the sacrament of baptism with excellent dispositions. Patrick, seeing his generosity towards God, did not hesitate to impose a severe penance upon him for the evil life he had led.

"Leave this place," he said, "and go to the sea-coast without weapons, without food, and wearing but one poor garment. Having reached the shore, lock thy feet in such iron fetters as hostages wear; throw the key into the sea, and embark in the smallest coracle thou canst find, leaving God to direct thy course by the winds and waves whithersoever He will. Where thou shalt land there remain, doing the high will of God."

At once MacCuill replied—

"All this I will do. But what is to become of this poor dead man?"

"He will come to life without difficulty," said Patrick; and at that moment he performed the miracle of raising Garvan from the dead.

Now there were at this time in the Isle of Man two holy missionaries, Conindri and Rumili, wonderful men, who were preaching God's word; and through their preaching the inhabitants believed and were baptized. When they saw MacCuill in his coracle cast upon their shore, they received him with charitable welcome, took off his fetters and attended to his needs. He glorified God by telling them of his marvellous conversion from a wicked life, of the penance imposed upon him by Patrick, and his own ready performance of it—

"Fierce chief no more, but soldier of the Cross."

They supplied the instruction that was lacking to him, and from them he learnt the precepts of the gospel and fulfilled them exactly. He spent the whole time of his life in the company of the two saints, and, when they died, he became their successor.

"This is 'MacCuill from the Sea,'" says the devout chronicler, "the illustrious Bishop and Prelate of Man. May his holy suffrages assist us!"

In this part of Ulster Patrick seems to have met with frequent opposition even at this late period of his career. It happened that two maidens had consecrated their virginity to God, but their king, Echaid, was determined to make them worship idols and to marry. Weary of their firm refusal to do his will he had them bound hand and foot and left upon the sea-shore that they might be drowned by the advancing tide.

The news of this persecution of Christian maidens was brought to Patrick that he might remonstrate with the tyrant whom no other dared to oppose. The Saint sent a message to Echaid entreating him to grant freedom to the virgins. But his intercession was of no avail, and Patrick, justly angry with Echaid, pronounced a doom upon him. No king should descend from him; of his race there would never be a troop large enough for an assembly or an army in Ulster; they would be scattered and dispersed, and his own life would be short and his end violent. But his brother, whom Echaid had smitten with a rod because he had begged him not to anger Patrick, should be a king and from him should descend kings and princes over Echaid's posterity and over the whole of Ulster.

At last the long series of missionary journeys came to an end. Patrick began to build a monastery in the district of Ross, apparently with the design of remaining there. But there came an angel to him and said—

"Not here hath it been granted to thee to abide."

"Where, then?" asked Patrick.

"Go to Armagh, in the north," said the angel.

"But verily," said Patrick, "the meadow below us here is most fair."

The angel conceded that this might be its name, even though Patrick must leave it. He said—

"Let this be its name 'Fair Meadow.' A pilgrim of the Britons will come and set up there, and it will be thine afterwards."

Patrick yielded to the angel's word.

"Deo gratias!" he said.

Nevertheless the Saint did not hasten to take up his abode in the place destined to be the primatial See of all Ireland. He rested at Ard-Patrick in Louth, the abode of his disciple and friend, the holy and learned Bishop Mochta, with whom he held pious discourse at a place called "Mochta's Flagstone." One day the angel placed a letter on the stone between them. Patrick taking the letter read it aloud. It ran as follows:—

> "Mochta, pious, believing,
> Let him bide in the place where he has set up,
> Patrick goes at his King's word
> To rest in smooth Armagh."

Chapter XII

The First Primate of All Ireland

UCH as our Saint would have desired to remain quietly for the rest of his life at Ard-Patrick, near his friend Mochta, the holy bishop of Louth, he could not resist this new call to move northward. All his life he had obeyed the impulses of the Holy Spirit, and he did not doubt that God was now urging him to take the last step in his long journey. Before he bade farewell to Mochta he placed under his care twelve lepers whom he had hitherto protected and provided for. Mochta willingly undertook the task and with his own hands carried their food to them every night.

An ancient queen of Ireland, Macha of the Golden Hair, gave her name to the hill, Ard-Macha, destined to be the site of St Patrick's primatial See. The descendants of Macha had been forced to leave their stronghold of Emania by the ancestors of the chieftain Daire, who now ruled the district. Daire was a wealthy and honourable man, by some historians called a king. He was well-disposed towards the new religion although we do not read that he ever became a Christian.

According to his usual custom, Patrick went straight to

the chieftain's fort and asked for an interview. The object he had in view was to obtain a portion of land on which to build a church.

"What place dost thou desire?" asked Daire.

"A place on this great hill," answered Patrick, pointing to the site of the future cathedral of Armagh.

"I will not give that," said Daire, for this "Ridge of the Willows," as it was then called, stood in a higher and stronger position than his own dun.

"Howbeit," he added, not wishing to appear churlish, "I will give a site for thy church in the strong rath below."

So Patrick had to be content for the present; and he "founded his cell there and remained therein a long time." He also built a church, and the graveyard surrounding it was fresh and grassy. One day two of Daire's horses were put to graze on this pleasant field. The desecration of consecrated ground was immediately punished by the death of the animals.

The servant in charge of the horses went to report the case to his master.

"This Christian," said he, "hath killed thy horses because they grazed on the grass that is growing around his church."

Daire was exceedingly wroth at this and bade his bondsmen attack Patrick and banish him out of the place. While they were preparing to obey his orders, Daire was seized with a sudden terrible illness which brought him to the point of death. His wife, thereupon, forbade the attack upon Patrick, and told her husband that his impending death was the result of his ungracious conduct towards the Saint. Moreover, she sent a messenger with a humble request for some water blessed by Patrick.

"If it had not been for the good offices of his wife," said Patrick, "Daire's resurrection from death would never have taken place."

So he blessed water and gave it to the servants, telling them that it was to be sprinkled over the horses and over Daire. On their return journey they passed the dead horses and did as Patrick had told them, whereupon the animals rose to their feet whole and sound and went home with the men. Daire's wife sprinkled the holy water over the sick man, who was immediately restored to health to the great joy of his family and friends.

In gratitude for his deliverance from death the chieftain sent Patrick as a present a beautiful copper cauldron which he had obtained from beyond the sea. The Saint received it with his usual "Deo Gratias!" for he acknowledged that all things came from God. Though he tells us in his "Confession" that he frequently restored what was given to him lest he should seem mercenary, this was an occasion when it seemed a mere matter of civility to accept the gift. When the messengers returned, Daire was anxious to know if his cauldron had been appreciated and asked what the Saint had said.

"He said 'gratzacham,' " they replied, imitating to the best of their ability the foreign phrase "Gratias agamus."

"That is a small reward for a goodly offering and a goodly cauldron," said Daire.

He commanded the servants to go and take the cauldron from Patrick and bring it back to him. The Saint was equally well pleased to be without the gift, and again thanked God for all his goodness to him. Once more Daire inquired what Patrick had said when deprived of the cauldron.

"He said the same thing as before," they replied, "that is 'gratzacham.' "

"That is a good word of his," said Daire, "gratzacham when it is offered to him, and gratzacham when it is taken from him. And for that good word let the cauldron be taken back to him."

Daire and his wife went with the servants who carried the cauldron to Patrick.

"This cauldron is thine," said the chief, "for thou art a man of steady purpose and of courage. And now thou shalt have that part of the Hill of the Willows which thou didst ask for. . Go and dwell there, for it is thine."

Whatever may be thought of the anecdotes of the horses and the cauldron "we may believe," says Professor Bury, "that Patrick won the respect of Daire as a man of firm character, and that for this reason Daire was induced to promote him to the higher site, granting him the land on the hill, with the usual reservation of the rights of the tribe. So it came about that Patrick and his household went up from their home at the foot of the hill and made another home on its summit."

It is remarkable that Daire, rude and uncultured as he seems to have been, gathered from the very meekness of Patrick the idea that he was a man of constancy and courage. During his missionary journeys the Saint had need to exercise all the energy of his forceful character and to call into play the supernatural assistance granted to him by God. As long as there was active work to be done he was bound, as the chosen instrument of God, to do it with might and main. But that work was now at an end. If he went to take possession of Armagh as his primatial See, it was solely because he was urged thereto by the Divine Will. The time had come for passive acquiescence and for entire detachment from earthly things.

Daire was welcome to give or to take away the cauldron, to give or to take away the land, just as God willed, and Patrick had ready his "Deo gratias!" in every case. Nevertheless, Daire was acute enough to perceive that this passivity in prosperity and in adversity was an effect of chastened strength, rather than, as might have been supposed from his age, of senile weakness. The Apostle had advanced from virtue to virtue and was now so united to God that self was, as it were, annihilated.

The right to the Hill of the Willows having been acquired, Patrick and his attendant clergy went in procession to the appointed spot. Daire, accompanied by the chief men of the district, came to do honour to the occasion and they stood reverently round about to watch the proceedings. A beautiful little incident occurred at this moment.

On the summit of the hill it happened that a doe was lying with her fawn just at the point where one of the altars was afterwards to stand. The spectators wished to seize the animals and kill them, but Patrick would by no means allow this to be done. Regardless of the interrupted ceremony he stooped and took up the fawn, placing it on his shoulder like the Good Shepherd who carries his newly found sheep. Followed by the doe he went towards the north until he reached a safe place, and there he let the fawn loose in a brake, where, says the chronicler, marvellous signs still happen.

"But," remarks Archbishop Healy, "the greatest sign of all has happened in our own time. For this northern hill, which in the time of St Patrick was a wooded brake, is now the site of the new cathedral of St Patrick, the largest and the most commanding church in Ireland.

"Patrick, who saw through the mystic veil of the future, no doubt saw, too, how that doe with her fawn was a figure of his own Church of Armagh, destined to be so often hunted and persecuted, 'so often doomed to death, yet fated not to die,' and he must have had a vision of the glory that awaited his church on that northern hill in the far distant ages. All the facts are typical of the history of the Church of Armagh, and it is clear that the ancient annalists who recorded them felt them to be such."

The plan of the new church was speedily made, and willing hands set to work and built it. As befitted its dignity it was larger than the ordinary churches erected by Patrick in Ireland. The Saint was assisted in his pastoral cares by Benignus, now freed from his duties of secretary, and coadjutor-bishop of Armagh. Daire may not have become a Christian, but we may suppose that his good wife embraced the faith, and we know that at least one of their children frequented the offices in the cathedral.

This was the Princess Ercnat who, as the romantic story tells, had been attracted by the beautiful voice and the sweet face of Benignus as he sang the holy office. The pagan maiden was so affected by not being able to obtain any notice from the Christian cleric that she fell ill and was at the point of death. Her mother came in anguish to Patrick, begging him to save her child.

The Saint blessed some water and sent Benignus to sprinkle it upon the patient. The end may be told in the words of Aubrey de Vere:

> "The maiden lay as dead; Benignus shook
> Dews from the font above her, and she woke
> With heart emancipate that outsoared the lark
> Lost in blue heavens. She loved the Spouse of souls,
> It was as though some child that, dreaming, wept
> Its childish playthings lost, awaked by bells,
> Bride-bells, had found herself a queen, new wed
> Unto her country's lord."

We may suppose that the maiden was restored by baptism, for we are told that she consecrated herself to God and became one of Patrick's embroideresses, of whom three, as the same poet sings,

> "Were daughters of three kings. The best and fairest.
> King Daire's daughter, Erenait by name."

Another of Patrick's embroideresses had come from a great distance, if we may believe the following story. The fame of the Saint had spread from Ireland to Britain, and thence to the continent, so that many pilgrims came to visit this great thaumaturgus of the West. It was an age of pilgrimages, and it was not, therefore, considered very wonderful that nine daughters of the King of the Lombards should come in a ship to see St Patrick and to obtain his advice. With a daughter of the King of Britain they tarried at a spot to the east of Armagh called after them "The Maidens' Hazel"; and they sent messengers to Patrick to ask whether they might go to him.

Now there were no nuns in the city of Armagh, so Patrick sent word that they were to go to a place called "The Champions' Ridge" and settle in a convent there. But he also foretold that three of them would die while at "The Maidens' Hazel," and this came to pass. One of them, moreover, Cruimtheris by name, was to live alone at Cengoba, the hillock to the east. Patrick provided for her simple wants, and she spent her time in working for the church and the altars, having, perhaps, been specially chosen on account of her skill in needlework.

> "When Patrick now was old and nigh to death,
> Undimmed was still his eye; his tread was strong;
> And there was ever laughter in his heart,
> And music in his laughter."

He saw to it that there was no time spent in idleness at Armagh. All were well occupied according to their talents— clearing the ground, building, planting orchards, sowing and reaping grain, copying manuscripts, and making sacred vessels and vestments for the service of the altar. And the soul of it all was the old man, spent with labours and drawing near his end; yet, nevertheless, quick of speech, bright of eye, energetic in action, dignified in bearing; the man who had baptized, instructed, ordained, and consecrated the bishops and clergy around him, not to speak of the thousands of souls scattered all over the island which bowed in loving submission to his primatial rule.

The story goes that the primacy of Armagh received special confirmation from heaven. One night Patrick's angel came and awoke him from sleep. The Saint in his humility at once thought that he had failed in some duty.

"Is there aught in which I am wont to offend God, or which has roused His anger against me?" he inquired.

"There is not," replied the angel, "and it hath been ordained for thee by God, if it seems good unto thee, that no one else shall have a share in Ireland save thee alone."

Once more Patrick proved his lack of ambition and his entire detachment from earthly things. He said—

"Verily, Sons of Life will come after me, and I desire that they should have honour from God after me in the land."

"In that thou showest thy charity," said the angel, "and God hath given all Ireland to thee, and every freeman that shall abide in Ireland shall be thine."

"I give God thanks," said Patrick, yielding at once with his unvarying formula, "Deo gratias!"

It is related that one day the men of Patrick's household were reaping a field, and as the weather was very warm they were exceedingly thirsty. On hearing of this the Saint sent to them a quantity of whey-water, but he recommended them to wait until the hour of vespers as it was a fast-day. Their master's simplest wish was to them a command, and so well was it observed that one of the men actually died of thirst rather than drink of the whey-water. Patrick was grievously afflicted when he heard of this heroic endurance, and the man who thus signalised himself holds his place in the annals of Armagh as "Colman the Thirsty."

It is evident from the chronicles that Patrick's nephew, Secundinus the bishop, known to the Irish as St Sechnall, was on terms of the most affectionate familiarity with his uncle. In spite of the intense reverence he felt towards the Saint he could not always resist the temptation of teasing him a little. One day Sechnall said to Patrick—

"When shall I make a panegyric to thee?"

"The time is not come," said Patrick, who had no desire for the praises of bards or poets.

"I did not ask thee if it should be made," said Sechnall, "for indeed it shall be made."

"If it must be made, then," said Patrick, "it is meet that it should be done quickly."

This he said because he knew that Sechnall would soon die, and indeed "he was the first bishop who went under the mould of Ireland."

So Sechnall set to work at the Latin hymn which still bears his name. In order, perhaps, to draw off the Saint's attention from what he was doing, Sechnall affected to say disparaging things about his uncle.

"Patrick is a good man," he whispered to one of the Armagh household, "Patrick is an excellent man, if only he were not one thing."

The rumour went round, and came to Patrick's ears. Pretending to be very angry, he called Sechnall and asked for an explanation.

"What is that one thing," said Patrick, "that thou saidst I did not fulfil?"

"O my father," replied Sechnall playfully, "I said this: Little dost thou preach of almsgiving."

"My little son," said Patrick, "if I fulfil not charity I am guilty of breaking God's commandments. God knows that it is for the sake of charity that I preach not almsgiving. For if I preached it I should not leave a yoke of two chariot-horses for any one of the saints in this island present or future; but unto me would be given all that is mine and theirs. For sons of life will come after me into this island and they will need their service from men."

When Sechnall had finished composing his hymn he went in search of Patrick who was travelling. They met in a pass on the mountain side and each blessed the other.

"I desire," said Sechnall, "that thou shouldst listen to a panegyric I have made for a certain man of God."

"I welcome the praise of a man of God's household," said his uncle, without suspicion. Having obtained this permission Sechnall began the hymn at the first line of the second stanza, omitting the first because it contained the words—

"Merita beati Patricii Episcopi"

which would have betrayed everything. When about half the hymn had been recited Patrick became restless, observing perhaps, the unusual expression on the faces of the brethren who stood around. Sechnall asked him why he was uneasy.

"Let us go to a quieter place," said Patrick, "there what remains can be recited."

As the uncle and nephew moved away out of earshot of the rest, Patrick said—

"How can a human being be greatest in the kingdom of heaven?" (for this was the meaning of the line—"Maximus namque in regno coelorum.")

"The superlative is here used for the positive," replied Sechnall, "or it is because he has surpassed most of the men of his own race."

"That is a good answer," said Patrick.

When they reached a quiet place Patrick, having prayed, sat down and listened to the remainder of the hymn. Then only did Sechnall read the first stanza, confirming Patrick in the suspicion he had already formed that he was himself the person eulogised. Indifferent now alike to praise and blame, he let the matter drop, only congratulating his nephew on his performance.

But Sechnall wished to profit by the opportunity. It was a custom of the Irish bards to sing complimentary verses in honour of their patrons and to be rewarded for doing so.

"I claim a guerdon for the hymn," said Sechnall.

The usual bargaining so dear to the storyteller's heart is here drawn out at wearisome length. Finally it was settled that whoever of the men of Ireland should recite this hymn, or even a portion of it, with a pure intention, should have the assistance of Patrick especially at the hour of death. Hence the hymn of St Secundinus became a very common prayer with the Irish and was considered most efficacious in every necessity both spiritual and temporal.

As the discourse between Patrick and his nephew drew to a close there came forward a pious couple, Berach and Brig, offering three curd cheeses and some butter to the Saint.

"This is for the little boys," said the woman, meaning the young ecclesiastical students in Patrick's school at Armagh.

"That is good of you," said Patrick, gratefully accepting the offering.

At this moment a foreign wizard approached and said mockingly—

"I will believe in thee if these cheeses are turned into stones."

Patrick's power had been sufficiently tested by the native wizards and it was long since he had been challenged. For the sake of the foreigner he now asked God to work this miracle. It was immediately done.

"Turn them again into cheeses," said the wizard irreverently.

The humble Saint obeyed without a word.

"Turn them again into stones," said the wizard, presuming on the venerable Saint's patience.

Patrick turned them into stones.

"Turn them back," said the wizard.

The power of God had been fully vindicated, and His

minister, though humble and patient, was not a juggler who could be commanded at will. In earlier days Patrick's indignation would have been roused, but now he simply said—

"Nay, but thus shall they remain in commemoration of the deed, until hither shall come a servant of God"—namely, St Dichuill.

Vanquished by so much charity and meekness, the scoffing wizard became a sincere convert to the Christian faith and was baptized by Patrick.

The zeal and love of the holy Primate embraced the whole island and all its inhabitants. We do not know at what date, but it was certainly towards the close of his life that the raid of the British chieftain, Coroticus, occurred. This cruel man was presumably a Christian, and yet he did not scruple to seize a number of newly-baptized persons and carry them off into slavery. Others in their white garments with the chrism of confirmation still gleaming on their foreheads were massacred.

"Therefore," says Patrick in his epistle to Coroticus, "in sadness and grief shall I cry aloud. O most lovely and loving brethren, and sons whom I begot to Christ, I cannot the number tell, what shall I do for you? I am not worthy to come to the aid of either God or men. The wickedness of the wicked hath prevailed against us."

The letter to Coroticus contained severe denunciations and was equivalent to an excommunication. It is unquestionably the work of St Patrick himself and as such is second in value only to the "Confession," which it resembles in style, and in its beginning "I, Patrick, a sinner and unlearned." Like the "Confession," also, it was written towards the close of his life.

"Now after these great marvels," says the chronicler, "the day of Patrick's death and of his going to heaven drew nigh." His affectionate heart was deeply attached to Armagh, the scene of his last labours for God, the church of his predilection and the school where he was training so many young clerics who were to continue his apostolic mission in Ireland. Once more he sang a pathetic little song—

> "I have chosen a place for my resurrection,
> My Church of Armagh
> I have no power over my freedom,
> It is bondage to the end.
> Armagh it is that I love,
> Its thorpe and hill are dear to me,
> My soul haunteth its fortress,
> But Emania of the heroes will be waste."

Then his angel came to him and said—

"Thy crozier shall be for ever in Armagh and great shall be the power and the dignity of thy Church."

It happened that Patrick was at Saul when he felt that his last hour was drawing near. At once "he began to go to Armagh that his resurrection might be therein." The Angel Victor came and warned him that in so doing he would be acting contrary to the will of God.

"It is not there," said Victor, "that thy resurrection hath been granted to thee. Go back to the place from which thou hast come, namely the Barn, for it is there thou shalt die and not in Armagh. It hath been granted to thee by God that thy dignity and thy pre-eminence, thy piety and thy teaching shall be in Armagh as if thou thyself wert alive therein."

And so it has ever been, for, says Archbishop Healy, "though false priests and ruthless foes desolated Patrick's royal city again and again, it has risen anew from its ashes. Patrick's power has never failed. Patrick's crozier has never been broken. His successors have been driven repeatedly from the royal hill, as the Popes have been driven from Rome; they have been hunted, imprisoned and slain; but the succession has not failed; the crozier was always there, as the angel foretold. And in our own time we have seen the great twin towers rise in pride and strength over Patrick's city, proclaiming to all the world that Patrick is still enthroned on Macha's Hill, clothed in larger glory, for the successor of Peter has robed his seat with the crimson of Rome, in which it was never draped before."

So Patrick made his last sacrifice and with a "Deo gratias" as ever on his lips he returned to Saul, to Dichu's Barn, where he had said his first Mass on the soil of Ireland. The Last Sacraments were given to him by Bishop Tassach of Raholp, whose church had been founded by the Saint himself. The Tripartite sums up Patrick's life and death in the following words:—

"Now after founding churches in plenty, after consecrating monasteries, after baptizing the men of Ireland, after great patience and after great labour, after destroying idols and images and after rebuking many kings who did not do his will, after ordaining three hundred and three score and ten bishops, and after ordaining three thousand priests, and folk of every grade in the church besides; after fasting and prayer: after mercy and clemency; after gentleness and mildness to the Sons of Life: after love of God and his neighbour, he received Christ's Body from Tassach the Bishop, and then he sent his spirit to Heaven."

Patrick's humility led him to speak in very different language of himself:—

"If I ever accomplished anything good," he says, "for the sake of my God Whom I love, I ask Him to grant that I may shed my blood with the strangers and the captives for His name's sake, even though I should want burial or my body should most miserably be divided limb from limb for the dogs and wild beasts, or that the fowls of the air should devour it." And if he, Patrick, the sinner and unlearned, has done any small thing in accordance with God's will, he begs that it will

Death of St. Patrick.

be attributed to the gift of God alone. "And this," he adds, "is my confession before I die."

The Saint's body was reverently wrapped in the winding-sheet made expressly for him by St Brigid and her nuns. It was then taken into the small church at Saul and kept there for twelve days before burial. The sad tidings flew from mouth to mouth and soon the whole island was aware of the loss of its saintly Apostle. Bishops and priests from every part of Ireland flocked towards Saul to be present at the obsequies.

But on the first night, we are told, the grief-stricken monks, weary with long watching, fell asleep around the dead body of their beloved master. Then the angels took up the spiritual canticles and continued them till morning, when crowds of clerics came with lighted tapers to watch and sing the office of the Church. When night came "an angelic radiance" mingled with the light of the tapers and torches and this continued during the twelve nights, or, as some say, for a year.

On the last day of the twelve the holy body was placed upon a bier and borne to Downpatrick where it was buried deep on the hillside, for there was great fear lest strife should arise as to its final resting-place. But the Saint, who had taught his children the lessons of peace, prevented them from taking up arms against each other on his account. Many are the stories told about the place and manner of Patrick's burial, but no man knows with certainty where his relics lie, and this Patrick himself obtained for the sake of peace. But his body will rise gloriously on the last day, when, as the Tripartite says, "it will shine like a sun in heaven, and when it will give judgment on the fruit of his preaching, even as Peter or Paul. It will abide thereafter in the union of patriarchs and prophets, in the union of the saints and holy virgins of the world, in the union of the apostles and disciples of Jesus Christ, in the union of the Church both of heaven and earth: in the union of the nine ranks of heaven that transgressed not, in the union of the Godhead and Manhood of God's Son, in the union that is nobler than any union, the union of the Trinity, Father, Son and Holy Ghost.

"I beseech God's mercy," concludes the chronicler, "through Patrick's intercession. May we all attain to that union! May we deserve it! May we dwell therein for ever and ever!" So:—

"Patrick, our Patriarch, died; and happy Feast
Is that he holds, by two short days alone
Severed from his of Hebrew Patriarchs last,
And chief. The holy house at Nazareth
He ruled benign, God's warder, with white hairs;
And still his feast, that silver star of March,
When snows afflict the hill, and frost the moor,
With temperate beam gladdens the vernal Church—
All praise to God, who draws that Twain so near!"

Appendix

Shrine of St. Patrick's Hand.

Appendix A

St Patrick's Hymn Before Tara

Called St Patrick's Breastplate, or The Deer's Cry

T Tara to-day, in this awful hour,
    I call on the Holy Trinity!
Glory to Him Who reigneth in power,
    The God of the elements, Father and Son,
    And Paraclete Spirit, which Three are the One,
      The ever-existing Divinity!

At Tara to-day I call on the Lord,
On Christ the Omnipotent Word,
Who came to redeem from Death and Sin
      Our fallen race;
      And I put and I place
The virtue that lieth and liveth in
      His Incarnation lowly,
      His Baptism pure and holy,
His life of toil, and tears and affliction,
His dolorous Death—His Crucifixion,
His Burial, sacred and sad and lone,
    His Resurrection to life again,
His glorious Ascension to Heaven's high Throne,
And, lastly, His future dread
    And terrible coming to judge all men
    Both the Living and Dead. . .

At Tara to-day I put and I place
  The virtue that dwells in the Seraphim's love,
And the virtue and grace
    That are in the obedience
    And unshaken allegiance
  Of all the Archangels and Angels above,
And in the hope of the Resurrection
To everlasting reward and election,
And in the prayers of the Fathers of old,
And in the truths of Prophets foretold,
And in the Apostles' manifold preachings,
And in the Confessors' faith and teachings,
And in the purity ever dwelling
  Within the Immaculate Virgin's breast,
And in the actions bright and excelling
  Of all good men, the just and the blest. . . .

At Tara to-day, in this fateful hour,
I place all Heaven with its power,
And the sun with its brightness,
And the snow with its whiteness,
And fire with all the strength it hath,
And lightning with its rapid wrath,
And the winds with their swiftness along their path,
And the sea with its deepness,
And the rocks with their steepness,
And the earth with its starkness—
    All these I place,
    By God's Almighty help and grace,
Between myself and the Powers of Darkness.

    At Tara to-day
    May God be my stay!
May the strength of God now nerve me!
May the power of God preserve me!
May God the Almighty be near me!
May God the Almighty espy me!
May God the Almighty hear me!
May God give me eloquent speech!
May the arm of God protect me!
May the wisdom of God direct me!
May God give me power to teach and to preach!

May the shield of God defend me!
May the host of God attend me,
    And ward me
Against the wiles of demons and devils,
    And guard me
Against the temptation of vices and evils,
Against the bad passions and wrathful will
  Of the reckless mind and the wicked heart,
Against every man who designs me ill,
    Whether leagued together or plotting apart!

    In this hour of hours,
    I place all those powers
Between myself and every foe
    Who threaten my body and soul
    With danger or dole
To protect me against the evils that flow
From lying soothsayers' incantations,
From the gloomy laws of the Gentile nations,
From heresy's hateful innovations,
From idolatry's rites and invocations,
    Be those my defenders,
  My guards against every ban,
And spells of smiths, and Druids, and women;
In fine, against every knowledge that renders
    The light Heaven sends us dim in
    The spirit and soul of Man!

    May Christ, I pray,
    Protect me to-day
Against poison and fire,
Against drowning and wounding,
That so, in His grace abounding,
    I may earn the Preacher's hire!

    Christ, as a light,
    Illumine and guide me!
Christ, as a shield,
O'ershadow and cover me!
Christ be under me! Christ be over me!
    Christ be beside me
    On left hand and right!

Christ be before me, behind me, about me!
Christ this day be within and without me!
Christ, the lowly and meek,
   Christ, the All-powerful, be
In the heart of each to whom I speak,
In the mouth of each who speaks to me!
     In all who draw near me,
      Or see or hear me!

At Tara to-day, in this awful hour,
   I call on the Holy Trinity!
Glory to Him Who reigneth in power,
The God of the elements, Father and Son,
And Paraclete Spirit, which Three are the One,
     The ever-existing Divinity!
Salvation dwells with the Lord,
With Christ, the Omnipotent Word,
From generation to generation.
Grant us, O Lord, Thy grace and salvation!

JAMES CLARENCE MANGAN.

Appendix B

The Confession of Saint Patrick

I PATRICK, a sinner, the rudest and least of all the faithful, and most contemptible to very many, had for my father Calpornius, a deacon, the son of Potitus, a priest, who lived in Bannaven Taberniae, for he had a small country-house close by, where I was taken captive when I was nearly sixteen years of age. I knew not the true God, and I was brought captive to Ireland with many thousand men, as we deserved; for we had forsaken God, and had not kept His commandments, and were disobedient to our priests, who admonished us for our salvation. And the Lord brought down upon us the anger of His Spirit, and scattered us among many nations, even to the ends of the earth, where now my littleness may be seen amongst strangers. And there the Lord showed me my unbelief, that at length I might remember my iniquities, and strengthen my whole heart towards the Lord my God, who looked down upon my humiliation, and had pity upon my youth and ignorance, and kept me before I knew him, and before I had wisdom or could distinguish between good and evil, and strengthened and comforted me as a father would his son.

Therefore I cannot and ought not to be silent concerning the great benefits and graces which the Lord has bestowed upon me in the land of my captivity, since the only return we can make for such benefits is, after God has reproved us, to extol and confess His wonders before every nation under heaven.

For there is no other God, nor ever was, nor shall be hereafter, except the Lord, the unbegotten Father, without beginning, by whom all things have their being, who upholds all things, as we have said; and His Son, Jesus Christ, whom, together with the Father, we testify to have always existed before the origin of the world, spiritually with the Father, ineffably begotten before every beginning; and by Him were the visible things made— was made man, death being overthrown, in the heavens. And he hath given Him all power over every name of things in heaven and earth and hell, that every tongue should confess to Him that Jesus Christ is Lord, and whose coming we expect ere long to judge the living and dead; who will render to every one according to his works; who hath poured forth abundantly on us both the gift of His Spirit and the pledge of immortality; who makes the faithful and obedient to become the sons of God and coheirs with Christ; whom we confess and adore one God in the Trinity of the holy Name. For He Himself has said by the prophet: "Call upon me in the day of thy trouble: I will deliver thee, and thou shalt magnify me." And again he says: "It is honorable to reveal and confess the works of God."

Although I am imperfect in many things, I wish my brothers and acquaintances to know my dispositions, that they may be able to understand the desire of my soul. I am not ignorant of the testimony of my Lord, who declares in the psalm: "Thou wilt destroy all that speak a lie." And again: "The mouth that belieth, killeth the soul." And the same Lord: "Every idle word that men shall speak, they shall render an account for it in the Day of Judgment." Therefore I ought, with great fear and trembling, to dread this sentence in that day when no one shall be able to withdraw or hide himself, but all must give an account, even of the least sins, before the judgment-seat of the Lord Christ.

Therefore, although I thought of writing long ago, I feared the censure of men, because I had not learned as the others who studied the sacred writings in the best way, and have never changed their language since their childhood, but continually learned it more perfectly, while I have to translate my words and speech into a foreign tongue; and it can be easily proved from the style of my writings how I am instructed in speech and learning, for the Wise Man says: "By the tongue wisdom is discerned, and understanding and knowledge and learning by the word of the wise." But what avails an excuse, however true, especially when accompanied with presumption? For I, in my old age, strive after that which I was hindered from learning in my youth. But who will believe me? And if I say what I have said before, that as a mere youth, nay, almost a boy in words, I was taken captive, before I knew what I ought to seek and to avoid. Therefore I blush to-day and greatly dread to expose my ignorance, because I am not able to express myself briefly, with clear and well-arranged words, as the spirit desires and the mind and intellect point out. But if it had been given to me as to others, I would not have been silent for the recompense; and although it may seem to some who think thus that I put myself forward with my ignorance and too slow tongue, nevertheless it is written, "The tongues of stammerers shall speak readily and plain"; how much more ought we to undertake this who are the epistle of Christ for salvation unto the ends of the earth, written in pure heart, if not with eloquence, yet with power and endurance, "not written with ink, but with the Spirit of the living God"; and again the Spirit testifies, "Husbandry, it was ordained by the Most High."

Therefore I undertook this work at first, though a rustic and a fugitive, and not knowing how to provide for the future; but this I know for certain: that before I was humbled, I was like a stone lying in deep mire, until He who is powerful came, and in his mercy raised me up, and indeed again succored and placed me in His part; and therefore I ought to cry out loudly, and thank the Lord in some degree for all his benefits, here and after, which the mind of man cannot estimate. Therefore be amazed, both great and small who fear God; rhetoricians and ye of the Lord, hear and enquire who aroused me, a fool, from the midst of those who seem to be wise, and skilled in the law, and powerful in speech and in all things, and hath inspired me (if indeed I be such) beyond others, though I am despised by this world, so that, with fear and reverence and without murmuring, I should faithfully serve this nation, to whom the charity of Christ hath transferred me, and given me for my life, if I shall survive; and that at last with humility and truth I should serve them.

In the measure, therefore, of the faith of the Trinity it behoves me to distinguish without shrinking from danger, and to make known the gift of God and everlasting consolation, and, without fear, confidently to spread abroad the name of God everywhere, so that after my death I may leave it to my Gallican brethren and to my sons, many thousands of whom I have baptized in the Lord. And I was neither worthy nor deserving that the Lord should so favor me, his servant, after such afflictions and great difficulties, after captivity, after many years, as to grant me such grace for this nation—a thing which, still in my youth, I had neither hoped for nor thought of.

But after I had come to Ireland, I was daily tending sheep, and I prayed frequently during the day, and the love of God, and His faith and fear, increased in me more and more, and the spirit was stirred; so that in a single day I have said as many as a hundred prayers, and in the night nearly the same; so that I remained in the woods, and on the mountain, even before the dawn, I was roused to prayer, in snow, and ice, and rain, and I felt no injury from it, nor was there any slothfulness in me, as I see now, because the spirit was then fervent in me. And there one night I heard a voice, while I slept, saying to me: "Thou dost fast well; fasting thou shalt soon go to thy country." And again, after a very short time, I heard a response, saying to me: "Behold, thy ship is ready." And the place was not near, but perhaps about two hundred miles distant, and I had never been there, nor did I know any one who lived there.

Soon after this, I fled, and left the man with whom I had been six years, and I came in the strength of the Lord, who directed my way for good; and I feared nothing until I arrived at that ship. And the day on which I came the ship had moved out of her place; and I asked to go and sail with them, but the master was displeased, and replied angrily: "Do not seek to go with us." And when I heard this, I went from them to go thither where I had lodged; and I began to pray as I went; but before I had ended my prayer, I heard one of them calling out loudly after me, "Come quickly, for these men are calling you"; and I returned to them immediately, and they began saying to me; "Come, we receive thee in good faith; make such friendship with us as you wish." And then that day I disdained to supplicate them, on account of the fear of God; but I hoped of them that they would come into the faith of Jesus Christ, for they were Gentiles; and this I obtained from them; and after three days, we reached land, and for twenty-eight days we journeyed through a desert, and their provisions failed, and they suffered greatly from hunger; and one day the master began to say to me: "What sayest thou, O Christian? Your God is great and all-powerful; why canst thou not, then, pray for us, since we are perishing with hunger, and may never see the face of man again?" And I said to them plainly: "Turn sincerely to the Lord my God, to whom nothing is impossible, that He may send us food on your way until ye are satisfied, for it abounds everywhere for Him." And with God's help it was so done; for, lo! a flock of swine appeared in the way before our eyes, and they killed many of them, and remained there two nights, much refreshed and filled with their flesh; for many of them had been left exhausted by the wayside. After this, they gave the greatest thanks to God, and I was honored in their eyes.

They also found wild honey, and offered me some of it, and one of them said: "This is offered in sacrifice, thanks be to God"; after this, I tasted no more. But the same night, while I was sleeping, I was strongly tempted by Satan (of which I shall be mindful as long as I shall be in this body), and there fell, as it were, a great stone upon me, and there was no strength in my limbs. And then it came into my mind, I know not how, to call upon Elias, and at the same moment I saw the sun rising in the heavens; and while I cried out Elias with all my might, behold! the splendor of the sun was shed upon me, and immediately shook from me all heaviness. And I believe that Christ my Lord cried out for me; and I hope that it will be so in the day of my adversity, as the Lord testifies in the Gospel: "It is not you that speak," etc.

Some time after, I was taken captive; and on the first night I remained with them I heard a divine response, saying: "You shall be two months with them"; and so it was. On the sixtieth night the Lord delivered me out of their hands, and on the road He provided for us food, and fire, and dry weather daily, until on the fourteenth day we all came. As I have above mentioned, we journeyed twenty-eight days through a desert, and on the night of our arrival we had no provisions left.

And again, after a few years, I was with my relations in Britain, who received me as a son, and earnestly besought me that then, at least, after I had gone through so many tribulations, I would go nowhere from them. And there I saw, in the midst of the night, a man who appeared to come from Ireland, whose name was Victoricus, and he had innumerable letters with him, one of which he gave to me; and I read the commencement of the epistle containing "The Voice of the Irish"; and as I read aloud the beginning of the letter, I thought I heard in my mind the voice of those who were near the wood of Focluti, which is near the western sea; and they cried out: "We entreat thee, holy youth, to come and walk still amongst us." And my heart was greatly touched, so that I could not read any more, and so I awoke. Thanks be to God that, after very many years, the Lord hath granted them their desire!

And on another night, whether in me or near me God knows, I heard eloquent words which I could not understand until the end of the speech, when it was said: "He who gave His life for thee is He who speaks in thee"; and so I awoke full of joy. And again, I saw one praying within me, and I was, as it were, within my body, and I heard, that is, above the inner man, and there he prayed earnestly with groans. And I was amazed at this, and marvelled, and considered who this could be who prayed in me. But at the end of the prayer it came to pass that it was a bishop, and I awoke and remembered that the apostle said: "Likewise the Spirit also helpeth our infirmity, for we know not what we should pray for as we ought, but the Spirit Himself asketh for us with unspeakable groanings." And again: "The Lord is our advocate, who also maketh intercession for us." [And when I was tried by some of my elders, who came and spoke of my sins as an objection to my laborious episcopate, I was on that day sometimes strongly driven to fall away here and for ever. But the Lord spared a proselyte and a stranger for His name's sake, and mercifully assisted me greatly in that affliction, because I was not entirely deserving of reproach. I pray God that they may not be found guilty of giving an occasion of sin; they found me after thirty years, and brought against me words that I had confessed before I was a deacon; from anxiety, with sorrow of mind, I told my dearest friend what I had done in my youth, in one day, nay, rather in one hour, because I was not then able to overcome. I know not, God knows, if I was then fifteen years of age, and from my childhood I did not believe in the living God, but remained in death and unbelief until I was severely chastised, and, in truth, I have been humbled by hunger and nakedness; and even now I did not come to Ireland of my own will until I was nearly worn out. But this proved a blessing to me, for I was thus corrected by the Lord, and he made me fit to be to-day that which was once far from my thoughts, so that I should care for the salvation of others, for at that time I had no thought even for myself.

And in the night of the day in which I was reproved for the things above mentioned, I saw in the night.] I saw in a vision of the night a writing without honor before me. And then I heard an answer saying to me, "We have heard with displeasure the face of the elect without a name." He did not say, "Thou hast badly seen," but "We have badly seen," as if he had there joined himself to me, as he said: "He that touches you is as he who toucheth the apple of my eye." Therefore I give thanks to Him who comforted me in all things that He did not hinder me from the journey which I had proposed, and also as regards my work which I had learned of Christ. But from this thing I felt no little strength, and my faith was approved before God and man.

Therefore I dare to say that my conscience does not reproach me now or for the future. I have the testimony of God now that I have not lied in the words I have told you. [But I feel the more grieved that my dearest friend, to whom I would have trusted even my life, should have occasioned this. And I learned from certain brethren that, before this defence, when I was not present, nor even in Britain, and with which I had nothing to do, that he defended me in my absence. He had even said to me with his own lips: "Thou art going to be given the rank of bishop," though I was not worthy of it. How, then, did it happen to him that afterwards, before all persons, good and bad, he should detract me publicly, when he had before this freely and gladly praised me? And the Lord, who is greater than all? I have said enough. Still, I ought not to hide the gift of God which he gave me in the land of my captivity, for I sought him earnestly then, and found him there, and He preserved me from all iniquity, I believe, through the indwelling of His Spirit, which worketh within me unto this day more and more. But God knows, if it were man who spoke this to me, I would perhaps be silent for the love of Christ.

Therefore I give unceasing thanks to my God, who preserved me faithful in the day of my temptation, so that I can to-day offer him sacrifice confidently—the living sacrifice of my soul to Christ my Lord, who preserved me from all my troubles, so that I may say to Him: "Who am I, O Lord! or what is my calling, that divine grace should have so wrought with me, so that to-day I can so rejoice amongst the nations, and magnify Thy name, wherever I am, not only in prosperity, but also in adversity?" and I ought to receive equally whatever happens to me, whether good or evil, giving God thanks in all things, who hath shown me that I should, undoubtingly, without ceasing, believe in Him who hath heard me though I am ignorant, and that I should undertake, in those days, so holy and wonderful a work, and imitate those of whom our Lord predicted of old that they should preach His Gospel to all nations for a testimony before the end of the world; which has been accomplished, as we have seen. Behold, we are witnesses that the Gospel has been preached to the limits of human habitation.]

But it is too long to detail my labors particularly, or even partially. I will briefly say how the good God often delivered me from slavery and from twelve dangers by which my soul was threatened, besides many snares, and what in words I cannot express, and with which I will not trouble my readers. But God knows all things, even before they come to pass [as he does me, a poor creature. Therefore the divine voice very often admonished me to consider whence came this wisdom, which was not in me, who neither knew God nor the number of my days. Whence did I obtain afterwards the great and salutary gift to know or love God, and to leave my country and my relations, although many gifts were offered to me with sorrow and tears. And I offended many of my seniors then against my will. But, guided by God, I yielded in no way to them— not to me, but to God be the glory, who conquered in me, and resisted them all; so that I came to the Irish people to preach the Gospel, and bear with the injuries of the unbelieving, and listen to the reproach of being a stranger, and endure many persecutions, even to chains, and to give up my freedom for the benefit of others. And if I be worthy, I am ready to give up my life unhesitatingly and most cheerfully for His name, and thus, if the Lord permit, I desire to spend it even until my death.]

For I am truly a debtor to God, who has given me so much grace that many people should be born again to God through me, and that for them everywhere should be ordained priests for this people, newly come to the faith, which the Lord took from the ends of the earth, as He promised formerly by His prophets: "Our fathers falsely prepared idols, and there is no profit in them, to thee the Gentiles come and will say." And again: "I have set thee to be the light of the Gentiles, that thou mayest be for salvation unto the utmost parts of the earth." And thus I wait the promise of Him who never fails, as He promises in the Gospel: "They shall come from the east and the west [from the north and from the south], and shall sit down with Abraham and Isaac and Jacob." So we believe that the faithful shall come from all parts of the world.

Therefore we ought to fish well and diligently; as the Lord taught and said: "Come ye after me, and I will make you fishers of men." And again: "Behold, saith the Lord, I send many fishers and many hunters," etc. Therefore we should, by all means, set our nets in such a manner that a great multitude and a crowd may be caught therein for God, and that everywhere there may be priests who shall baptize and exhort a people who so need it and desire it; as the Lord teaches and admonishes in the Gospel, saying: "Going, therefore, teach ye all nations, baptizing them in the name of the Father and of the Son and of the Holy Ghost, even to the consummation of the world." And again: "Go ye into the whole world, and preach the Gospel to every creature; he that believeth and is baptized shall be saved, but he that believeth not shall be condemned." The rest are examples. [And again: "This Gospel of the kingdom shall be preached in the whole world for a testimony to all nations, and then shall the consummation come." And again, the Lord, speaking by the prophet, says: "And it shall come to pass in the last days, saith the Lord, that I will pour out my spirit upon all flesh, and your sons and your daughters shall prophesy, your old men shall dream dreams, and your young men shall see visions. Moreover, upon my servants and handmaids in those days I will pour forth my spirit, and they shall prophesy." And Osee saith: "And I will say to that which was not my people: Thou art my people: and to her who hath not found mercy; and they shall say; Thou art my God. And in the place where I said to them, You are not my people, it shall be said to them, Ye are the sons of the living God."]

Wherefore behold how in Ireland they who never had the knowledge of God, and hitherto only worshipped unclean idols, have lately become the people of the Lord, and are called the sons of God. The sons of the Scoti and the daughters of princes are seen to be monks and virgins of Christ. [And there was one blessed Irish maiden, of adult age, noble and very beautiful, whom I baptized, and after a few days she came to us for a reason, and gave us to understand that she had received a command from God, and was informed that she was to become a virgin of Christ, and to draw near to God. Thanks be to God, six days after this she most excellently and eagerly entered on this state of life, which all the virgins of God now adopt, even against the will of their parents, even enduring reproaches and persecution from them, and notwithstanding they increase in number; and as for those who are born again in this way, we know not their number, except the widows and those who observe continency. But those who are in slavery are most severely persecuted, yet they persevere in spite of terrors and threats. But the Lord has given grace to many of my handmaids, for they zealously imitate him as far as they are able.

Therefore, though I could have wished to leave them, and had been ready and very desirous to go to Britannia, as if to my country and parents, and not that alone, but to go even to Gallia, to visit my brethren, and to see the face of my Lord's saints; and God knows that I desired it greatly. But I am bound in the spirit, and he who witnesseth will account me guilty if I do it, and I fear to lose the labor which I have commenced—and not I, but the Lord Christ, who commanded me to come and be with them for the rest of my life; if the Lord grants it, and keeps me from every evil way, that I should not sin before him. But I hope that which I am bound to do, but I trust not myself as long as I am in this body of death, for he is strong who daily tries to turn me from the faith, and from the sincere religious chastity to Christ my Lord, to which I have dedicated myself to the end of my life, but the flesh, which is in enmity, always draws me to death—that is, to unlawful desires, that must be unlawfully gratified—and I know in part that I have not led a perfect life like other believers. But I confess to my Lord, and do not blush before him, because I tell the truth, that from the time I knew him in my youth the love of God and his fear increased within me, and until now, by the favor of the Lord, I have kept the faith.

Let him who pleases insult and laugh at me; I will not be silent, neither do I conceal the signs and wonders that the Lord hath shown to me many years before they took place, as he who knew all things even before the world began. Therefore I ought to give thanks to God without ceasing, who often pardoned my uncalled-for folly and negligence, who did not let his anger turn fiercely against me, who allowed me to work with him, though I did not promptly follow what was shown me and what the Spirit suggested; and the Lord had compassion on me among thousands and thousands, because he saw my good-will; but then I knew not what to do, because many were hindering my mission, and were talking behind my back, and saying: "Why does he run into danger among enemies who know not God?" This was not said with malice, but because they did not approve of it, but, as I now testify, because of my rusticity, you understand; and I did not at once recognize the grace which was then in me, but now *I know I should have known before.*

Therefore I have simply related to my brethren and fellow-servants who have believed me why I have preached and still preach to strengthen and confirm your faith. Would that you also might aim at higher things and succeed better. This shall be my glory, because a wise son is the glory of his father. You know and God knows how I have lived among you from my youth up, both faithful in truth and sincere in heart; also, I have given the faith to the people among whom I dwell, and I will continue to do so. God knows I have not overreached any of them, nor do I think of it, because of God and his Church, lest I should excite persecution for them and all of us, and lest the name of the Lord should be blasphemed through me; for it is written, "Woe to the man through whom the name of the Lord is blasphemed." For though I am unskilled in names, I have endeavored to be careful even with my Christian brethren, and the virgins of Christ, and devout women, who freely gave me gifts, and cast of their ornaments upon the altar; but I returned them, though they were offended with me because I did so. But I, for the hope of immortality, guarded myself cautiously in all things, so that they could not find me unfaithful, even in the smallest matter, so that unbelievers could not defame or detract from my ministry in the least.

But when it happened that I baptized so many thousand men, did I expect even half a "screpall" from them? Tell me, and I will return it to you. Or when the Lord ordained clergy through my humility and ministry, did I confer the grace gratuitously? If I asked of any of them even the value of my shoe, tell me, and I will repay you more. I rather spent for you as far as I was able; and among you and everywhere for you I endured many perils in distant places, where none had been further or had ever come to baptize, or ordain the clergy, or confirm the people. By the grace of the Lord I labored freely and diligently in all things for your salvation. At this time also I used to give rewards to kings, whose sons I hired, who travelled with me, and who understood nothing but [to protect] me and my companions. And on one day they wished to kill me; but the time had not come yet; but they put me in irons, and carried off all we possessed. But on the fourteenth day the Lord released me from their power, and what was ours was restored to us through God and through the friends we had before secured.

You know how much I expended on the judges in the districts which I visited most frequently. For I think I paid them not less than the hire of fifteen men, that you might have the benefit of my presence, and that I might always enjoy you in the Lord. I do not regret it, nor is it sufficient for me. I still spend, and will still spend, for your souls.] Behold, I call God to witness on my soul that I do not lie, neither that you may have occasion, nor that I hope for honor from any of you; sufficient for me is the honor of truth. But I see that now in the present world I am greatly exalted by the Lord; and I was not worthy nor fit to be thus exalted, for I know that poverty and calamity are more suitable for me than riches and luxury. But even Christ the Lord was poor for us.

Truly, I, a poor and miserable creature, even if I wished for wealth, have it not; neither do I judge myself, because I daily expect either death, or treachery, or slavery, or an occasion of some kind or another. [But I fear none of these things, relying on the heavenly promise; for I have cast myself into the hands of the omnipotent God, who rules everywhere; as the prophet says: "Cast thy care upon the Lord, and He shall sustain thee."

Behold, now I commend my soul to my most faithful God, whose mission I perform, notwithstanding my unworthiness; but because He does not accept persons, and has chosen me for this office, to be one of the least of His ministers. "What shall I render to Him for all the things that He hath rendered to me?" But what shall I say or promise to my Lord? For I see nothing unless He gives Himself to me; but He searches the heart and reins, because I ardently desire and am ready that He should give me to drink His cup, as He has permitted others to do who have loved Him. Wherefore may my Lord never permit me to lose His people whom He has gained in the ends of the earth. I pray God, therefore, that He may give me perseverance, and that He may vouchsafe to permit me to give

Him faithful testimony for my God until my death. And if I have done anything good for my God, whom I love, I beseech Him to grant to me that with those proselytes and captives I may pour out my blood for His name, even if my body should be denied burial, and be miserably torn limb from limb by dogs or fierce beasts, or that the birds of heaven should devour it. I believe most certainly that if this should happen to me, I have gained both soul and body; for it is certain that we shall rise one day in the brightness of the sun—that is, the glory of Christ Jesus our Redeemer—as sons of God but as joint heirs with Christ, and to become conformable to His image.

For that sun which we see rises daily for us; but it will not rule or continue in its splendor for ever, and all who adore it shall suffer very miserably. But we who believe in and adore the true sun, Christ, who will never perish, neither he who shall do His will, but even as Christ shall abide for ever, who reigns with God the Father Almighty, and with the Holy Spirit, before the ages, and now, and for ever and ever. Amen.

Behold, again and again, I shall briefly declare the words of my confession. I testify in truth and in joy of heart, before God and His holy angels, that I never had any occasion, except the Gospel and its promises, for returning to that people from whom I had before with difficulty escaped.]

But I beseech those who believe in and fear God, whoever may condescend to look into or receive this writing, which Patrick, the ignorant sinner, has written in Ireland, that no one may ever say, if I have ever done or demonstrated anything, however little, that it was my ignorance. But do you judge, and let it be believed firmly, that it was the gift of God. And this is my confession before I die.

Thus far is what Patrick wrote with his own hand; he was translated to heaven on the seventeenth of March.

Appendix C

St Patrick's Epistle to Coroticus

 PATRICK, a sinner and unlearned, have been appointed a bishop in Ireland, and I accept from God what I am. I dwell amongst barbarians as a proselyte and a fugitive for the love of God. He will testify that it is so. It is not my wish to pour forth so many harsh and severe things; but I am forced by zeal for God and the truth of Christ, who raised me up for my neighbors and sons, for whom I have forsaken my country and parents, and would give up even life itself, if I were worthy. I have vowed to my God to teach these people, though I should be despised by them, to whom I have written with my own hand to be given to the soldiers to be sent to Coroticus—I do not say to my fellow-citizens, nor to the fellow-citizens of pious Romans, but to the fellow-citizens of the devil, through their evil deeds and hostile practices. They live in death, companions of the apostate Scots and Picts, blood-thirsty men, ever ready to redden themselves with the blood of innocent Christians, numbers of whom I have begotten to God and confirmed in Christ.

On the day following that in which they were clothed in white and received the chrism of neophytes, they were cruelly cut up and slain with the sword by the above mentioned; and I sent a letter by a holy priest, whom I have taught from his infancy, with some clerics, begging that they would restore some of the plunder or the baptized captives; but they laughed at them. Therefore I know not whether I should grieve most for those who were slain, or for those whom the devil insnared into the eternal pains of hell, where they will be chained like him. For whoever commits sin is the slave of sin, and is called the son of the devil.

Wherefore let every man know who fears God that they are estranged from me, and from Christ my God, whose ambassador I am—these patricides, fratricides, and ravening wolves, who devour the people of the Lord as if they were bread; as it is said: "The wicked have dissipated thy law," wherein in these latter times Ireland has been well and prosperously planted and instructed. Thanks be to God, I usurp nothing; I share with these whom He hath called and predestinated to preach the Gospel in much persecution, even to the ends of the earth. But the enemy hath acted invidiously towards me through the tyrant Coroticus, who fears neither God nor His priests whom He hath chosen, and committed to them the high, divine power: "Whomsoever they shall bind on earth shall be bound in heaven."

I beseech you, therefore, who are the holy ones of God and humble of heart, that you will not be flattered by them, and that you will neither eat nor drink with them, nor receive their alms, until they do penance with many tears, and liberate the servants of God and the baptized hand-maids of Christ, for whom he was crucified and died. "He that offereth sacrifice of the goods of the poor, is as one that sacrificeth the son in the presence of the father." "Riches, he saith, which the unjust accumulate shall be vomited forth from his belly, the angel of death shall drag him away, he shall be punished with the fury of dragons, the tongue of the adder shall slay him, inextinguishable fire shall consume him." Hence, "Woe to those who fill themselves with things which are not their own." And "what doth it profit a man if he gain the whole world and suffer the loss of his soul?" It were too long to discuss one by one, or to select from the law, testimonies against such cupidity. Avarice is a mortal sin. "Thou shall not covet thy neighbor's goods." "Thou shall not kill." The homicide cannot dwell with Christ. "He who hateth his brother is a murderer," and "and he who loveth not his brother abideth in death." How much more guilty is he who hath defiled his hands with the blood of the sons of God, whom He hath recently acquired in the ends of the earth by our humble exhortations!

Did I come to Ireland according to God or according to the flesh? Who compelled me? I was led by the Spirit, that I should see my relatives no more. Have I not a pious mercy towards that nation which formerly took me captive? According to the flesh, I am of noble birth, my father being a Decurio. I do not regret or blush for having bartered my nobility for the good of others. I am a servant in Christ unto a foreign people for the ineffable glory of eternal life, which is in Christ Jesus my Lord; though my own people do not acknowledge me: "A prophet is without honor in his own country." Are we not from one stock, and have we not one God for our Father? As He has said: "He that is not with me is against me, and he that gathereth not with me scattereth." Is it not agreed that one pulleth down and another buildeth? I seek not my own.

Not to me be praise, but to God, who hath put into my heart this desire that I should be one of the hunters and fishers whom, of old, God hath announced should appear in the last days. I am reviled—what shall I do, O Lord? I am greatly despised. Lo! thy sheep are torn around me, and plundered by the above-mentioned robbers, aided by the soldiers of Coroticus: the betrayers of Christians into the hands of the Picts and Scots are far from the charity of God. Ravening wolves have scattered the flock of the Lord, which, with the greatest diligence, was increasing in Ireland; the sons of the Irish and the daughters of kings who are monks and virgins of Christ are too many to enumerate. Therefore the oppression of the great is not pleasing to thee now, and never shall be.

Who of the saints would not dread to share in the feasts or amusements of such persons? They fill their houses with the spoils of the Christian dead, they live by rapine, they know not the poison, the deadly food, which they present to their friends and children; as Eve did not understand that she offered death to her husband, so are all those who work evil: they labor to work out death and eternal punishment.

It is the custom of the Christians of Rome and Gaul to send holy men to the Franks and other nations, with many thousand solidi, to redeem baptized captives. You who slay them, and sell them to foreign nations ignorant of God, deliver the members of Christ, as it were, into a den of wolves. What hope have you in God? Whoever agrees with you, or commands you, God will judge him. I know not what I can say, or what I can speak more of the departed sons of God slain cruelly by the sword. It is written: "Weep with them that weep." And again: "If any member suffers anything, all the members suffer with it." Therefore the Church laments and bewails her sons and daughters, not slain by the sword, but sent away to distant countries, where sin is more shameless and abounds. There free-born Christian men are sold and enslaved amongst the wicked, abandoned, and apostate Picts.

Therefore I cry out with grief and sorrow. O beautiful and well-beloved brethren and children! whom I have brought forth in Christ in such multitudes, what shall I do for you? I am not worthy before God or man to come to your assistance. The wicked have prevailed over us. We have become outcasts. It would seem that they do not think we have one baptism and one Father, God. They think it an indignity that we have been born in Ireland; as He said: "Have ye not one God? Why do ye each forsake his neighbor?" Therefore I grieve for you—I grieve, O my beloved ones! But, on the other hand, I congratulate myself I have not labored for nothing—my journey has not been in vain. This horrible and amazing crime has been permitted to take place. Thanks be to God, ye who have believed and have been baptized have gone from earth to paradise. Certainly, ye have begun to migrate where there is no night or death or sorrow; but ye shall exult like young bulls loosed from their bonds and tread down the wicked under your feet as dust.

Truly, you shall reign with the apostles and prophets and martyrs, and obtain the eternal kingdom, as He hath testified, saying: "They shall come from the east and the west, and shall sit down with Abraham and Isaac and Jacob in the kingdom of heaven." Without are dogs, and sorcerers, and murderers, and liars, and perjurers, and they shall have their part in the everlasting lake of fire. Nor does the apostle say without reason: "If the just are scarcely saved, where shall the sinner, the impious, and the transgressor of the law appear?" Where will Coroticus and his wicked rebels against Christ find themselves when they shall see rewards distributed amongst the baptized women? What will he think of his miserable kingdom, which shall pass away in a moment, like clouds or smoke, which are dispersed by the wind? So shall deceitful sinners perish before the face of the Lord, and the just shall feast with great confidence with Christ, and judge the nations, and rule over unjust kings, for ever and ever. Amen.

I testify before God and His angels that it shall be so, as He hath intimated to my ignorance. These are not my words that I have set forth in Latin, but those of God and the prophets and apostles, who never lied: "He that believeth shall be saved, but he that believeth not shall be condemned."

God hath said it. I entreat whosoever is a servant of God that he be a willing bearer of this letter, that he be not drawn aside by any one, but that he shall see it read before all the people in the presence of Coroticus himself, that, if God inspire them, they may some time return to God, and repent, though late; that they may liberate the baptized captives, and repent for their homicides of the Lord's brethren; so that they may deserve of God to live and to be whole here and hereafter. The peace of the Father, and of the Son, and of the Holy Ghost. Amen.

INDEX

Additional titles available from

ST. AUGUSTINE ACADEMY PRESS

Books for the Traditional Catholic

TITLES BY MOTHER MARY LOYOLA:

Blessed are they that Mourn
Confession and Communion
Coram Sanctissimo (Before the Most Holy)
First Communion
First Confession
Forgive us our Trespasses
Hail! Full of Grace
Heavenwards
Holy Mass/How to Help the Sick and Dying
Home for Good
Jesus of Nazareth: The Story of His Life Written for Children
The Child of God: What comes of our Baptism
The Children's Charter
The Little Children's Prayer Book
The Soldier of Christ: Talks before Confirmation
Welcome! Holy Communion Before and After

TALES OF THE SAINTS:

A Child's Book of Saints by William Canton
A Child's Book of Warriors by William Canton
Illustrated Life of the Blessed Virgin by Rev. B. Rohner, O.S.B.
Legends & Stories of Italy by Amy Steedman
Mary, Help of Christians by Rev. Bonaventure Hammer
The Book of Saints and Heroes by Lenora Lang
Saint Patrick: Apostle of Ireland
The Story of St. Elizabeth of Hungary by William Canton

Check our Website for more:

www.staugustineacademypress.com

Lightning Source UK Ltd.
Milton Keynes UK
UKHW040632240521
384271UK00001B/160